THE CASE AGAINST
STANDARDIZED TESTING

THE CASE AGAINST STANDARDIZED TESTING

Raising the Scores, Ruining the Schools

Alfie Kohn

HEINEMANN
Portsmouth, NH

Heinemann

361 Hanover Street
Portsmouth, NH 03801–3912
www.heinemann.com

Offices and agents throughout the world

Library of Congress Cataloging-in-Publication Data
Kohn, Alfie.
    The case against standardized tests : raising the scores, ruining the schools / by Alfie Kohn.
       p. cm.
    Includes bibliographical references and index.
    ISBN 0-325-00325-4
    1. Achievement tests—United States. 2. Educational tests and measurements—United States. I. Title
LB3060.3 K64 2000
371.26'2'0973—dc21

                                           00-057245

Editor: Lois Bridges
Cover photo: John Willkes
Author photo: Jason Threlfall
Cover design: Catherine Hawkes/Cat & Mouse Design
Manufacturing: Louise Richardson

Printed in the United States of America on acid-free paper
10 09 08　　　**VP**　　　**11 12 13 14**

For my new son, Asa—
May his Apgar score be his last

CONTENTS

Much of the material in this book has been adapted from *The Schools Our Children Deserve: Moving Beyond Traditional Classrooms and "Tougher Standards"* (1999). Permission to do so has generously been granted by its publisher, Houghton Mifflin. Readers interested in broader issues of teaching and learning—as well as the "tougher standards" sensibility that underlies standardized testing—are invited to consult that book.

•

I am grateful for the comments and suggestions on this manuscript offered by Monty Neill and Danny Miller, as well as for the consistently professional, responsive, and friendly assistance offered by the entire crew at Heinemann. In particular, my editor, Lois Bridges, an estimable educator in her own right, talked me into this project and then proceeded to make it a pleasure for me—and to make the result better for you.

Standardized testing has swelled and mutated, like a creature in one of those old horror movies, to the point that it now threatens to swallow our schools whole. Of course, on the late, late show no one ever insists that the monster is really doing us a favor by making its victims more "accountable." In real life, plenty of people need to be convinced that these tests do not provide an objective measure of learning or a useful inducement to improve teaching, that they are not only unnecessary but highly dangerous. This book was written to challenge those who defend the tests.

Other readers are already well aware of what is being sacrificed in the drive to raise scores, but they may find it helpful to have a few facts or research results at their fingertips, a quotable phrase or a set of answers to commonly asked questions. This book was written to assist those who oppose the tests.

Still others want for neither reasons nor rhetoric; what they lack is the requisite sense of urgency or the belief that they can make a difference. This book was written to energize and encourage those who have resigned themselves to the tests.

The more we learn about standardized testing, particularly in its high-stakes incarnation, the more likely we are to be appalled. And the more we are appalled, the more inclined we will be to do what is necessary to protect our children from this monster in the schools.

MEASURING WHAT MATTERS LEAST

Is it my imagination, or are we spending an awful lot of time giving kids standardized tests?

It's not your imagination. While previous generations of American students have had to sit through tests, never have the tests been given so frequently and never have they played such a prominent role in schooling. Exams used to be administered mostly to decide where to place kids or what kind of help they needed; only recently have scores been published in the newspaper and used as the primary criteria for judging children, teachers, and schools—indeed, as the basis for flunking students or denying them a diploma, deciding where money should be spent, and so on. Tests have lately become a mechanism by which public officials can impose their will on schools, and they are doing so with a vengeance.

This situation is also unusual from an international perspective. "Few countries today give these formal examinations to students before the age of sixteen or so," two scholars report.[1] In the U.S., we subject children as young as *six* to standardized exams, despite the fact that almost all experts in early childhood education condemn this practice. And it isn't easy to find other countries that give multiple-choice tests to students of any age.[2]

In short, our children are tested to an extent that is unprecedented in our history and unparalleled anywhere else in the world. Rather than seeing this as odd, or something that needs to be defended, many of us have come to take it for granted. The result is that most of today's discourse about education has been reduced to a crude series of monosyllables: "Test scores are too low. Make them go up."

So what accounts for this?

Well, different people have different motivations. For some, a demand for tests seems to reflect a deliberate strategy for promoting traditional, "back-to-basics" instruction. (Whether or not that's the intent, it's often the consequence of an emphasis on standardized test scores.) Other people, meanwhile, are determined to cast public schools in the worst possible light as a way of paving the way for the privatization of education. After all, if your goal was to serve up our schools to the marketplace, where the point of reference is what maximizes profit rather than what benefits children, it would be perfectly logical for you to administer a test that many students would fail in order to create the impression that public schools were worthless.

Not everyone has ulterior motives for testing, of course. Some people just insist that schools have to be held "accountable," and they don't know any other way to achieve that goal. Even here, though, it's worth inquiring into the sudden, fierce demands for accountability. The famous *Nation at Risk* report released by the Reagan Administration in 1983 was part of a concerted campaign—based on exaggerated and often downright misleading evidence[3]—to stir up widespread concerns about our schools and, consequently, demands for more testing.

There's another built-in constituency: the corporations that manufacture and score the exams, thereby reaping enormous profits (on revenues estimated at nearly a quarter of a *billion* dollars in 1999, and continuing to grow rapidly). More often than not, these companies then turn around and sell teaching materials designed to raise scores on their own tests. The worst tests are often the most appealing to school systems: It is fast, easy, and therefore relatively inexpensive to administer a multiple-choice exam that arrives from somewhere else and is then sent back to be graded by a machine at lightning speed. There is little incentive to replace these tests with more meaningful forms of assessment that require human beings to evaluate the quality of students' accomplishments. "Efficient tests tend to drive out less efficient tests, leaving many important abilities untested—and untaught."[4]

Testing allows politicians to show they're concerned about school achievement and serious about getting tough with students and teachers. Test scores offer a quick-and-easy—although, as we'll see, by no means accurate—way to chart progress. Demanding high scores fits nicely with the use of political slogans like "tougher standards" or "accountability" or "raising the bar."

If the public often seems interested in test results, it may be partly because of our cultural penchant for attaching numbers to things. Any aspect of learning (or life) that appears in numerical form seems reassuringly scientific; if the numbers are getting larger over time, we must be making progress. Concepts such as intrinsic motivation and intellectual exploration are difficult for some minds to grasp, whereas test scores, like sales figures or votes, can be calculated and tracked and used to define success and failure. Broadly speaking, it is easier to measure efficiency than effectiveness, easier to rate how well we're doing something than to ask whether what we're doing makes sense. Not everyone realizes that the process of coming to understand ideas in a classroom is not always linear or quantifiable—or, in fact, that "measurable outcomes may be the least significant results of learning."[5]

But don't we need an objective measure of achievement?

This question is much more complicated than it may appear. Is objectivity really a desirable—or a realistic—goal? Presumably, an "objective" assessment is one that's not dependent on subjective factors such as the beliefs and values of different individuals; everyone would have to agree that something was good or bad. But disagreement is a fact of life, and it isn't necessarily something to be transcended. You and I will inevitably differ in our judgments about politics and ethics, about the quality of the movies we see and the meals we eat. It is odd and troubling that in educating our children "we expect a different standard of assessment than is normal in the rest of our lives."[6]

Too much standardization suggests an effort to pretend that evaluations aren't ultimately judgments, that subjectivity can be overcome. This is a dangerous illusion. Testing specialists always seem to be chasing the holy grail of "interrater reliability," but there's no reason to expect that people will always see eye-to-eye about the value of what students have done. If they do, that suggests either that they have obediently set aside their own judgments in order to rigidly apply someone else's criteria, or that the assessment in question is fairly superficial. For example, it's easier to get agreement on whether a semicolon has been used correctly than on whether an essay represents clear thinking. The quest for objectivity may lead us to measure students on the basis of criteria that are a lot less important.[7]

For the sake of the argument, though, let's assume that objective assessments are both possible and desirable. The critical point is that *standardized tests do not provide such objectivity*. It's easy to assume otherwise when a precise numerical score has been assigned to a student or school. But the testing process is nothing at all like, say, measuring the size or weight of an object. The results may sound scientific, but they emerge from the interaction of two sets of human beings: the invisible adults who make up the questions and the rows of kids, scrunched into desks, frantically writing (or filling in bubbles).

First, we need to know about the content of the test. Are we measuring something important? One can refer to it as "objective" in the sense that it's scored by machines, but people wrote the questions (which may be biased or murky or stupid) and people decided to include them on the exam. Reasonable doubts often can be raised about which answers ought to be accepted, even at the elementary school level, where you might expect the questions to be more straightforward. Thus, to read narrative accounts of students who think through a given question and arrive at a plausible answer— only to learn that the answer has been coded as incorrect[8]— is to understand the limits of these putatively objective assessment instruments.

suspicious

The significance of the scores becomes even more dubious once we focus on the experience of students. For example, test anxiety has grown into a subfield of educational psychology, and its prevalence means that the tests producing this reaction are not giving us a good picture of what many students really know and can do. The more a test is made to "count"—in terms of being the basis for promoting or retaining students, for funding or closing down schools—the more that anxiety is likely to rise and *the less valid the scores become.*

Then there are the students who take the tests but don't take them seriously. A friend of mine remembers neatly filling in those ovals with his pencil in such a way that they made a picture of a Christmas tree. (He was assigned to a low-level class as a result, since his score on a single test was all the evidence anyone needed of his capabilities.) Even those test-takers who are not quite so creative may just guess wildly, fill in ovals randomly, or otherwise blow off the whole exercise, understandably regarding it as a waste of time. In short, it may be that a good proportion of students either couldn't care less about the tests, on the one hand, or care so much that they choke, on the other. Either way, the scores that result aren't very meaningful. Anyone who can relate to these descriptions of what goes through the minds of real students on test day ought to think twice before celebrating a high score, complaining about a low one, or using standardized tests to judge schools.

Even if they're not "objective," though, wouldn't you agree that we need some way to tell which students are ready for the world of work? It's just not realistic to think we can eliminate testing.

The more you're concerned about what's "realistic," the more critical you should be of standardized tests. How many jobs demand that employees come up with the right answer on the spot, from memory, while the clock is ticking? (I can think of one or two, but they're the exceptions that prove the rule.) How often are we forbidden to ask coworkers for help, or to depend on a larger organization for support—even in a society that worships self-sufficiency? And when someone is going to judge the quality of your work, whether you are a sculptor, a lifeguard, a financial analyst, a professor, a housekeeper, a refrigerator repairman, a reporter, or a therapist, how common is it for you to be given a secret pencil-and-paper exam? Isn't it far more likely that the evaluator will look at examples of what you've already done, or perhaps watch you perform your normal tasks? To be consistent, those educational critics who indignantly insist that schools should be doing more to prepare students for the real world ought to be demanding an end to these artificial exercises called standardized tests.

Including the college admission tests, the SATs and ACTs?

Ideally, yes. These tests are not very effective as predictors of future academic performance, even in the freshman year of college, much less as predictors of professional success. They're not good indicators of thinking or aptitude; the verbal section is basically just a vocabulary test. (The "A" in SAT used to stand for Aptitude until the Educational Testing Service gave up this pretense. Now "SAT" doesn't stand for anything—in more ways than one.) They're not necessary for deciding who should be admitted to college. No such exams are used in Canada, for example, and several hundred U.S. colleges and universities no longer require applicants to take them.[9]

But these tests are not our primary concern here. It's far more worrisome that even students who don't plan to continue their schooling after high school, and even students who are much too young to be thinking about college are subjected to a barrage of standardized tests that don't provide much useful information.

The results of these tests must tell us something.

The main thing they tell us is how big the students' houses are. Research has repeatedly found that the amount of poverty in the communities where schools are located, along with other variables having nothing to do with what happens in class-rooms, accounts for the great majority of the difference in test scores from one area to the next.[10] To that extent, tests are sim-ply not a valid measure of school effectiveness. (Indeed, one educator suggested that we could save everyone a lot of time and money by eliminating standardized tests and just asking a single question: "How much money does your mom make? . . . OK, you're on the bottom."[11]) Only someone ignorant or dishonest would present a ranking of schools' test results as though it told us about the quality of teaching that went on in those schools when, in fact, it primarily tells us about socio-economic status and available resources. Of course, knowing what really determines the scores makes it impossible to defend the practice of using them as the basis for high-stakes decisions.

But socioeconomic status isn't everything. Within a given school, or group of students of the same status, aren't there going to be vari-ations in the scores?

Sure. And among people who smoke three packs of cigarettes a day, there are going to be variations in lung cancer rates. But that doesn't change the fact that smoking is the factor most powerfully associated with lung cancer.

Still, let's put wealth aside and just focus on the content of the tests themselves.[12] The fact is that they usually don't assess the skills and dispositions that matter most. They tend to be contrived exercises that measure how much students have man-aged to cram into short-term memory. Even the exceptions—questions that test the ability to reason—generally fail to offer students the opportunity "to carry out extended analyses, to solve open-ended problems, or to display command of com-plex relationships, although these abilities are at the heart of higher-order competence," as Lauren Resnick, one of our lead-ing cognitive scientists, put it.[13]

Part of the problem rests with an obvious truth whose impli-cations we may not have considered: These tests care only about whether the student got the right answer. To point this out is not to claim that there is no such thing as a right answer; it is to observe that right answers don't necessarily signal understanding, and wrong answers don't necessarily signal the absence of understanding. Most standardized tests ignore the process by which students arrive at an answer, so a miss is as good as a mile and a minor calculation error is interchangeable with a major failure of reasoning.

The focus on right answers also means that most, if not all, of the items on the test were chosen precisely because they have unambiguously correct solutions, with definite criteria for determining what those solutions are and a clear technique for getting there. The only thing wrong with these questions is that they bear no resemblance to most problems that occupy people in the real world.[14]

You're making some sweeping statements here. What subjects are you talking about? Reading? Math?

You pick. What generally passes for a test of reading comprehension is a series of separate questions about short passages on random topics. These questions "rarely examine how students interrelate parts of the text and do not require justifications that support the interpretations"; indeed, the whole point is the "quick finding of answers rather than reflective interpretation."[15]

In mathematics, the story is much the same. An analysis of the most widely used standardized math tests found that only 3 percent of the questions required "high level conceptual knowledge" and only 5 percent tested "high level thinking skills such as problem solving and reasoning."[16] Typically the tests aim to make sure that students have memorized a series of procedures, not that they understand what they are doing. They also end up measuring knowledge of arbitrary conventions (such as the accepted way of writing a ratio or the fact that "<" means "less than") more than a capacity for logical thinking. Even those parts of math tests that have names like "Concepts and Applications" are "still given in multiple-choice format, are computational in nature, and test for knowledge of basic skills through the use of traditional algorithms."[17]

The parts of standardized exams that deal with science or social studies, meanwhile, typically amount to nothing more than a test of obscure facts and definitions. They aren't designed to tell who has learned to think like a scientist or an historian; they're designed to tell who can recite the four stages of mitosis or the four freedoms mentioned by Franklin Roosevelt. As the president of the National Academy of Sciences has remarked, questions that focus on "excruciatingly boring material" not only fail to judge students' capacity to reason but wind up driving away potential future scientists.[18]

Are you saying the tests are too hard?

Sometimes they are. Plenty of successful adults would fail the high school exit exams used in many states—and might not even do all that well on some of the tests given to fourth graders. But the real problem isn't the difficulty level, per se. It's the fact that these tests are geared to a different, less sophisticated kind of knowledge. It's not just that the tests are often ridiculously hard; it's that they're simply ridiculous. They don't capture what most of us, upon reflection, would say it means to be a well-educated person.

Two math educators offer a good example from the Massachusetts test for high school students. The question reads as follows:

n 1 2 3 4 5 6
t_n 3 5
The first two terms of a sequence, t_1 and t_2, are shown above as 3 and 5. Using the rule: $t_n = t_{n-1} + t_{n-2}$, where n is greater than or equal to 3, complete the table.

This is actually just asking the test taker to add 3 and 5 to get 8, then add 5 and 8 to get 13, then add 8 to 13 to get 21, and so on.

The problem simply requires the ability to follow a rule; there is no mathematics in it at all. And many tenth-grade students will get it wrong, not because they lack the mathematical thinking necessary to fill in the table, but simply because they haven't had experience with the notation. Next year, however, teachers will prep students on how to use formulas like $t_n = t_{n-1} + t_{n-2}$, more students will get it right, and state education officials will tell us that we are increasing mathematical literacy.[19]

Even if the tests are imperfect, don't top students still do the best?

That depends on what you mean by "top students." If you mean those who are most interested in learning and most likely to think deeply, then the answer may surprise you. Although these findings haven't been widely publicized, studies of students of different ages have found *a statistical association between high scores on standardized tests and relatively shallow thinking.* One of these studies classified elementary school students as "actively" engaged in learning if they went back over things they didn't understand, asked questions of themselves as they read, and tried to connect what they were doing to what they had already learned; and as "superficially" engaged if they just copied down answers, guessed a lot, and skipped the hard parts. It turned out that the superficial style was positively correlated with high scores on the Comprehensive Test of Basic Skills (CTBS) and Metropolitan Achievement Test (MAT).[20] Similar findings have emerged from studies of middle school and high school students.[21]

These are only statistical relationships, you understand—significant correlations, but not absolute correspondences. There are plenty of students who think deeply *and* score well on tests. There are also plenty of students who do neither. But as a rule, good standardized test results are more likely to go hand in hand with a shallow approach to learning than with deep understanding. By virtue of their design (more about which later), "most tests *punish* the thinking test-taker"[22]—to the point that some teachers advise their students, in effect, to dumb themselves down so they can do better on the tests.[23]

Perhaps this is why, as Piaget pointed out years ago, "Anyone can confirm how little the grading that results from examinations corresponds to the final useful work of people in life."[24] But never mind their inability to predict what students will be able to do later; they don't even capture what students can do today. In fact, we might say that such tests fail in two directions at once. On the one hand, they overestimate what some students know: Those who score well often understand very little of the subject in question. Students may be able to find a synonym or antonym for a word without being able to use it properly in a sentence. They may have memorized the steps of comparing the areas of two figures without really understanding geometric principles at all. On the other hand, standardized tests *under*estimate what others can do because, as any teacher can tell you, very talented students often get low scores. For example, there are "countless cases of magnificent student writers whose work was labeled as 'not proficient' because it did not follow the step-by-step sequence of what the test scorers (many of whom are not educators, by the way) think good expository writing should look like."[25]

Consider a fifth grade boy who, researchers found, could flawlessly march through the steps of subtracting $2\frac{5}{6}$ from $3\frac{1}{3}$, ending up quite correctly with $\frac{3}{6}$ and then reducing that to $\frac{1}{2}$. Unfortunately, successful performance of this final reduction does not imply understanding that the two fractions are equivalent. In fact, this student remarked in an interview that $\frac{1}{2}$ was larger than $\frac{3}{6}$ because "the denominator is smaller so the pieces are larger." Meanwhile, one of his classmates, whose answer had been marked wrong because it hadn't been expressed in the correct terms, clearly had a better grasp of the underlying concepts. Intrigued, these researchers proceeded to interview a number of fifth graders about another topic (division) and discovered that 41 percent had memorized the process without really understanding the idea, while 11 percent understood the concept but made minor errors that resulted in getting the wrong answers. A standardized test therefore would have misclassified more than half of these students.[26]

THE WORST TESTS

Surely, though, all *standardized tests aren't this bad.*

No, some are even worse. The most damaging testing programs are characterized by certain readily identifiable features, beginning with the use of exams that are mostly multiple choice. "I don't think there's any way to build a multiple-choice question that allows students to show what they can do with what they know," says Roger Farr, professor of education at Indiana University[27]—a statement all the more remarkable given that Farr personally helped to write a number of standardized tests. The reasons should be obvious. Students are unable to *generate* a response; all they can do is recognize one by picking it out of four or five answers provided by someone else. They can't even *explain* their reasons for choosing the answer they did. Obviously some sort of remembering, calculating, or thinking has to be done to figure out which answer is "most appropriate," but other sorts of mental operations (such as organizing information or constructing an argument) are pretty much excluded by the format. No matter how clever or tricky the questions are, a multiple-choice test simply "does not measure the same cognitive skills as are measured by similar problems in free-response form," as one expert explained in a now-classic article. The difference between the two formats (which is to say, the limits of multiple-choice questions) really shows up when the idea is to measure "complex cognitive problem-solving skills."[28]

Well, I'm relieved. My state's exam has a lot of multiple-choice questions on it, but at least it has some open-response items, too.

Unfortunately, even essay questions often leave a lot to be desired. They may require students to analyze a dull chunk of text, cough up obscure facts, or produce cogent opinions on command about some bland topic—hardly an authentic assessment of meaningful learning. What's more, these questions are often scored on the basis of imitating a contrived model (such as a cookie-cutter five-paragraph essay) rather than tapping real communication or thinking skills. Preparing kids to turn out high-scoring essays can *inhibit* the quality of their writing.

The way these exams are graded raises even more concerns. For example, the essays written by students in many states are not evaluated by educators; they are shipped off to a company in North Carolina where low-paid temp workers spend no more than two or three minutes reading each one. "There were times I'd be reading a paper every ten seconds," one former scorer told a reporter. Sometimes he "would only briefly scan papers before issuing a grade, searching for clues such as a descriptive passage within a narrative to determine what grade to give. 'You could skim them very quickly . . . I know this sounds very bizarre, but you could put a number on these things without actually reading the paper,'" said this scorer, who, like his coworkers, was offered a "two hundred dollar bonus that kicked in after eight thousand papers."[29]

In short, we can't assume that an essay test is a valid measure of important things. But we can be reasonably certain that a multiple-choice test *isn't*.

All right, what else is relevant besides the format of the questions?

First, beware of tests that are **timed.** If students must complete an examination within a specified period, this means that a premium is placed on speed as opposed to thoughtfulness or even thoroughness. If one small part of the test were timed, this would indicate that the ability to do things quickly and under pressure was one of several valued attributes. But if the entire exam must be taken under the gun, the logical inference is that this ability is prized above others.

Second, you should be worried if tests are given **frequently.** It is neither necessary (in terms of collecting information) nor desirable (in terms of improving the quality of instruction) to test students year after year after year. This practice is generally connected to grade-by-grade performance standards, and they, in turn, reflect the assumption that all students must learn at the same pace. As a descriptive premise, this is out of step with developmental reality; as a prescriptive formula, it ensures that those who require more time to learn will be branded as failures. The uniformity implied in grade-level standards and testing emphasizes the speed (measured in months or years) at which students must master a set curriculum—an interesting echo of the disproportionate emphasis on speed (measured in minutes or hours) reflected in the use of timed exams.

Third, be prepared to protest if tests are given **to young children.** Students below fourth grade simply should not be subjected to standardized examinations—first, because it is difficult, if not impossible, to devise such an assessment in which they can communicate the depth of their understanding;[30] and second, because skills develop rapidly and differentially in young children, which means that expecting all second graders to have acquired the same skills or knowledge creates unrealistic expectations and leads to one-size-fits-all (which is to say, poor) teaching.[31] In fact, "what test-makers are measuring for some children" is not their cognitive capacities so much as their "ability to sit in the same place for a certain amount of time."[32]

Finally, look out for tests that are **"norm-referenced."**

I've heard that term a lot, but I've never understood exactly what it means.

Robert Glaser coined the term "norm-referenced test" (NRT) many years ago to refer to tests that "provide little or no information about . . . what the individual can do. They tell that one student is more or less proficient than another, but do not tell how proficient either of them is with respect to the subject matter tasks involved."[33] The most common norm-referenced tests are the Iowa and Comprehensive Tests of Basic Skills (ITBS and CTBS), and the Stanford, Metropolitan, and California Achievement Tests (SAT, MAT, and CAT). In contrast to a test that's "criterion-referenced," which means it compares each individual to a set standard, one that's norm-referenced compares each individual to everyone else, and the result is usually (but not always) reported as a percentile.

Think for a moment about the implications of this. No matter how many students take an NRT, no matter how well or poorly they were taught, no matter how difficult the questions are, the pattern of results is guaranteed to be the same: Exactly 10 percent of those who take the test will score in the top 10 percent, and half will always fall below the median. That's not because our schools are failing; that's because of what the word *median* means. A good score on an NRT means "better than other people," but we don't even know how much better. It could be that everyone's actual scores are all pretty similar, in which case the distinctions between them are meaningless, rather like saying I'm the tallest person on my block even though I'm only half an inch taller than the shortest person on my block.

More important, even if the top 10 percent did a *lot* better than the bottom 10 percent, that still doesn't tell us anything at all about how well they did in absolute terms, such as how many questions they got right. Maybe everyone did reasonably well; maybe everyone blew it. We don't know. Norm-referenced tests cannot tell us—indeed, were never designed to tell us—how much of a body of knowledge a student learned or a school taught. To try to use them for those purposes is, in the words of W. James Popham, a leading authority, "like measuring temperature with a tablespoon."[34] Yet NRTs *are* used for exactly those purposes all across the United States, often by people who should know better.

14

Norm-referenced tests are not about assessing excellence; they are about sorting students (or schools) into winners and losers. The animating spirit is not "How well are they learning?" but "Who's beating whom?" The latter question doesn't provide useful information because the only thing that really counts is how many questions on a test were answered correctly (assuming they measured important knowledge). By the same token, the news that your state moved up this year from thirty-seventh in the country to eighteenth doesn't tell us whether its schools are really improving: for all you know, the schools in your state are in worse shape than they were last year, but those in other states slid even further.[35]

Even that isn't the whole story. When specialists sit down to construct an NRT, they're not interested in making sure the questions cover what is most important for students to know. Rather, their goal is to include questions that some test-takers—not all of them, and not none of them—will get right. They don't *want* everyone to do well on the test. The ultimate objective, remember, is not to evaluate how well the students were taught, but to separate them, to get a range of scores. If a certain question is included in a trial test and almost everyone gets it right—or, for that matter, if almost no one gets it right—that question will likely be tossed out. Whether it is reasonable for kids to get it right is irrelevant.[36]

Even if these tests aren't as informative as we've been led to believe, what's the harm of seeing how kids stack up against one another?

Given that scores from NRTs are widely regarded as if they contained meaningful information about how our children (and their schools) are doing, they are not only dumb but dangerous. And the harm ramifies through the whole system in a variety of ways. First, these tests contribute to the already pathological competitiveness of our culture, where we come to regard others as obstacles to our own success—with all the suspicion, envy, self-doubt, and hostility that rivalry entails. The process of assigning children to percentiles helps to ensure that schooling is more about triumphing over everyone else than it is about learning.[37]

Second, because every distribution of scores contains a bottom, it will always appear that some kids are doing terribly.

That, in turn, reinforces a sense that the schools are failing. Worse, it contributes to the insidious assumption that some children just can't learn—especially if the same kids always seem to show up below the median. (This conclusion, based on a misunderstanding of statistics, is then defended as "just being realistic.") Parents and teachers may come to believe this falsehood, and so too may the kids themselves. They might figure: No matter how much I improve, everyone else will probably get better too, and I'm always going to be at the bottom. So why bother trying? Conversely, a very successful student, trained to believe that rankings are what matter, may be confident of remaining at the top and therefore have no reason to do as well as possible. (Excellence and victory, after all, are two completely different goals.) For both groups of students, it is difficult to imagine a more powerful demotivator than norm-referenced testing.

There's more: The questions that "too many" students will answer correctly probably are those that deal with the content teachers have been emphasizing in class because they judged it to be important. So NRTs are likely to include a lot of trivial stuff that *isn't* emphasized in school because that material is useful for distinguishing one student from another. Therefore, teachers and administrators who are determined to outsmart the test—or who are under pressure to bring up their school's rank—may try to adjust the curriculum in order to bolster their students' scores. (More about this later.) But if the tests emphasize relatively unimportant knowledge that's designed for sorting, then "teaching to the test" isn't going to improve the quality of education. It may have exactly the opposite effect.

These basic facts should be understandable to almost everyone, yet the mind boggles at the reality that our children continue to be subjected to tests like the ITBS and the current version of the Stanford Achievement Test (the SAT-9), which are both destructive and ridiculously ill-suited to the purposes for which they are used.

So I can relax if my state's test isn't norm-referenced?

All else being equal, a test is certainly less damaging if it's not set up as a zero-sum game. Nevertheless, these tests may be treated as though they *were* norm-referenced. That can happen if parents or students aren't helped to understand that a score of 80 percent refers to the proportion of questions answered correctly, leaving them to assume that it refers to a score better than 80 percent of the other test-takers.[38] Worse yet, criterion-referenced tests may be turned *into* the norm-referenced kind if newspapers publish charts showing how every school or district ranks on the same exam, thereby calling attention to what is least significant. (One expert on testing suggests that if newspapers insist on publishing such a chart, they should at least place it where it belongs, in the sports section.)[39]

Finally, even if your state officials know better than to subject kids to NRTs, your local officials may not. Plenty of school districts are making students take norm-referenced (mostly multiple-choice) tests on top of the ones mandated by the state.

It's starting to sound as though you don't like any standardized tests.

Again, not all tests are equally bad. The least useful and most damaging testing program would be one that uses (1) a norm-referenced exam in which students must answer (2) multiple-choice questions in a (3) fixed period of time—and must do so (4) repeatedly, beginning when they are (5) in the primary grades. But remember: Even testing programs that avoid some or all of these pitfalls are likely to be problematic to the extent they measure mere memorization or even test-taking skills. In any case, *all* standardized tests tend to ignore the most important characteristics of a good learner, to say nothing of a good person. Here's a list offered by educator Bill Ayers, although you might just as well make up your own:

> Standardized tests can't measure initiative, creativity, imagination, conceptual thinking, curiosity, effort, irony, judgment, commitment, nuance, good will, ethical reflection, or a host of other valuable dispositions and attributes. What they can measure and count are isolated skills, specific facts and functions, the least interesting and least significant aspects of learning.[40]

Beyond their ineffectiveness as assessments, note that the act of administering (and emphasizing the results of) standardized tests can communicate some pointed lessons about the nature of learning. Because there is a premium placed on remembering facts, children may come to think that this is what really matters—and they may even come to develop a "quiz show" view of intelligence that confuses being smart with knowing a lot of stuff. Because the tests are timed, students may be encouraged to see intelligence as a function of how quickly people can do things. Because the tests often rely on a multiple-choice format, students may infer "that a right or wrong answer is available for all questions and problems" in life and that "someone else already knows the answer to [all these questions], so original interpretations are not expected; the task is to find or guess the right answer, rather than to engage in interpretive activity."[41]

Two other features of standardized tests also may teach dubious lessons even as they detract from the tests' usefulness. First, they're given to individuals, not to groups, and helping one another is regarded as a serious offense. Not only is there no measure of the capacity to cooperate effectively, or even to assimilate other people's ideas into your own, but precisely the opposite message is communicated: Only what you can do alone is of any value. "We have been so convinced of the notion that intellect is an isolated, individual quality that we utterly lack the procedures or the psychometrics to study students' performances in group situations," as Dennie Wolf and her colleagues put it.[42]

Second, the content of these tests is kept secret. Given their nature, this is hardly surprising, but look at it this way: What does it say about an approach to assessment that it can be done only by playing "Gotcha!"? Tests "that continually keep students in the dark are built upon procedures with roots in pre-modern traditions of legal proceedings and religious inquisitions."[43] Apart from raising stress levels, the kind of evaluation where students aren't allowed to know in advance what they'll be asked to do suggests a heavy emphasis on memorization. It also has the practical effect of preventing teachers from reviewing the test with students after it's over and using it as a learning tool.

I'm sorry, but I just don't see how you could have a standardized test that didn't *have right answers, or wasn't secret or timed or whatever.*

You probably couldn't. That's my point. Many of the problems identified here are inherent to standardized testing. But here is a very different question: Could you devise a way of figuring out how well students are learning, or teachers are teaching, that didn't have these features? As we'll see on pp. 41–50, this question does have an answer. But it's critical that we frame the issue in these broader terms so that this becomes our point of departure. Only then are we free to look beyond—and avoid the problems created by—standardized tests.

BURNT AT THE HIGH STAKES

Do most people in the field of education recognize the problems you've described here?

There are no data on this, but my impression is that the people who work most closely with kids are the most likely to understand the limits of standardized tests. An awful lot of teachers—particularly those who are very talented—have what might be described as a dislike/hate relationship with testing. But support for testing seems to grow as you move away from the students, going from teacher to principal to central office administrator to school board member to state board member, state legislator, and governor. Those for whom classroom visits are occasional photo opportunities are most likely to be big fans of testing and to offer self-congratulatory sound bites about the need for accountability.

But what happens when teachers or students explain that they'd rather pursue other kinds of learning, that they don't care about scores? Doesn't this lead the people in charge to rethink the value of the tests?

To the contrary, most of them have responded by saying, in effect, "Well, then, we'll *force* you to care about the scores!" This they have done in several ways: first, by making sure the tests are given frequently, raising their visibility among teachers and students; second, by publishing the scores and encouraging the public to see them as indicators of school quality—even hoping that bad results might serve as a kind of "public shaming" that will pressure educators to do anything necessary to crank up their scores.

Finally, officials have responded by using an assortment of bribes and threats to coerce everyone into concentrating on the test results. If the scores are high, the bribes may include bonuses for teachers and schools. Students, meanwhile, may receive food, tickets to theme parks or sporting events, exemptions from in-class final exams, and even substantial scholarships.[44] The threats include loss of funding or accreditation for schools, while students may be held back a year or denied a high school diploma if they don't test well, regardless of their overall academic record. Collectively, these kinds of tactics are known as "high-stakes" testing.

Some of these methods do seem harsh, but doesn't it make sense to "put some teeth" into the standards?

Not unless you think the way to improve education is by biting people. These policies are unwise for many reasons, beginning with the deficiencies of the tests themselves. Always remember that it is the results on those deeply flawed exams that determine who gets rewarded or punished. In fact, some states and cities are actually making rewards and punishments contingent on the results of *norm-referenced* tests (e.g., the ITBS in Chicago, the Stanford-9 in California), a policy that has rightly been described as educational malpractice.

Before we look at the real-world effects of high-stakes testing, it's worth considering that the approach is simply unfair. It holds people "accountable" for factors over which they have little control, which is as pointless as it is cruel. For example, low scores—in absolute and especially in relative terms—are to a large extent due to social and economic factors, as we've already seen. Those factors include the resources available to the school as well as the level of affluence of the community in which the school is located. But even to the extent that the scores do reflect school experience, that experience is hardly limited to the current year. Thus, it seems difficult to justify holding a fourth-grade teacher accountable for her students' test scores when those scores reflect all that has happened to the children before they even arrived at her class.

Then there is the possibility for error, which becomes far more disturbing when high stakes are attached to test results. It seems as though every month or so one of the big test publishers, Harcourt Brace, CTB/McGraw Hill, or Riverside, makes some sort of mistake scoring exams. In one such episode, New York City officials ordered 8,600 students to attend remedial summer school on the basis of a scoring error on the CTBS. Still more unsettling is the fact that standardized tests have inaccuracies built into them. Even when they are scored correctly, and even when they meet conventional standards for reliability, many children will be misclassified because of the limits of test accuracy. A Stanford University researcher calculated that a student whose hypothetical "real achievement" is at the fiftieth percentile will actually score within five percentage points of that level only about 30 percent of the time on the SAT-9 math exam and 42 percent of the time on the reading exam.[45] Yet rewards and punishments hinge on such scores as though they were perfect measures of achievement.

But the basic idea of giving people an incentive to improve makes sense, doesn't it?

Not really. A detailed explanation of this point would take us too far afield,[46] but suffice it to say that rewards and punishments can never succeed in producing more than temporary compliance, and even that result is achieved at a substantial cost.

People can sometimes be dissuaded from doing certain things if they are threatened with a punitive consequence, but this tends to create a climate of fear, which, in turn, generates anger and resentment. It also leads people to act more cautiously. As a rule, human beings are less likely to think creatively when they perceive themselves to be under threat. (Hence the wry humor of a sign posted in some offices and classrooms, which could be the motto of the contemporary "tougher standards" movement: THE BEATINGS WILL CONTINUE UNTIL MORALE IMPROVES.) When individuals are threatened with the deprivation of money, status, autonomy, or something else they value, any temporary effect in the desired direction—desired, that is, by the individual with the power to issue these threats—is usually more than offset by the demoralization that occurs.

The use of punishments and threats is sometimes justified on the grounds that, however disagreeable, it succeeds in "motivating" people. But this argument is based on the simplistic and ultimately faulty assumption that motivation consists of a single entity that people possess to a greater or lesser degree: Threaten someone with an aversive consequence unless she does *x*, and her motivation to do it will rise. Decades of psychological theory and research have challenged this view by demonstrating that there are different kinds of motivation. Moreover, it appears that *the kind matters more than the amount*. Psychologists typically distinguish between "intrinsic" and "extrinsic" motivation, depending upon whether one sees a task as valuable in its own right or merely a means to an end. It's obvious to most of us that these two forms of motivation are qualitatively different. It's also reasonably clear that intrinsic motivation is more desirable and more potent over the long haul. No amount of extrinsic motivation to do something can compensate for an absence of genuine enthusiasm. Adults who consistently do excellent work, and students whose learning is most impressive, are usually those who love what they do, not those who see what they do as a way to escape a punishment (such as losing out on a bonus or being forced to repeat a grade).

Furthermore, extrinsic motivation is not merely different or inferior; it's corrosive. That is, it tends to undermine intrinsic motivation. Under most real-life conditions, these two forms of motivation are likely to be reciprocally related. Someone acting to avoid a punishment is apt to lose interest in that which he was threatened into doing. Teaching and learning alike come to be seen as less appealing when someone has a gun to your head.

But what if no punishments are used? What if someone is just offered a reward for doing a good job?

That, too, is a form of extrinsic motivation. In fact, there's even more evidence about the destructive effects of rewards than there is about punishments. Scores of studies have demonstrated that *the more people are rewarded for doing something, the more they tend to lose interest in whatever they had to do to get the reward.* Thus, the intrinsic motivation that is so vital to quality—to say nothing of quality of life—often evaporates in the face of extrinsic incentives, be they carrots or sticks.[47]

Rewards and punishments are sometimes described as though they were opposites—and as though they exhausted the available strategies for effecting change. Thus, discussions are framed in terms of which one is preferable. The truth of the matter is that the two are mirror images of one another, variations on a single theme. Both represent ways of doing things *to* people, as distinct from working *with* people. Indeed, one reason that extrinsic inducements are likely to be counterproductive is that they are widely, and usually correctly, construed as tactics of control. This is more overt in the case of punishment ("Do this or here's what will be done to you") but no less true in the case of rewards ("Do this and you'll get that"). The more desirable the incentive, the more that using it to get people to act in a particular way is likely to backfire, particularly when the goal is something deeper, more complex, or longer lasting than temporary compliance.

The more familiar one becomes with the psychological research, the sillier one realizes it is to use rewards or punishments as a way of "motivating" people to accomplish important goals.

But most of that research didn't deal with high-stakes testing, right?

That's correct. Here my point has been only that the psychological underpinning of high-stakes testing—the use of incentives, per se—is flawed. Even if we got the details right, the whole approach is likely to do far more harm than good.

Still, I'm tempted to reply that there are a lot of incompetent teachers out there. Don't we have to resort to stronger measures to make them improve?

Certainly it's true that not all teachers—or representatives of any profession, for that matter—are inspiring and impressive. But the relevant question is whether a "doing to" strategy is likely to be more effective at helping them improve than is a "working with" strategy. (A related question is which approach is likely to attract more talented people to the field of education.)

All of the research showing that rewards and punishments are at best ineffective, and more commonly counterproductive, challenges the assumption that people can be bribed or threatened into getting better at what they do. Granted, it's often hard to craft a feasible alternative for staff development, but that doesn't argue for persisting with a heavy-handed tactic that clearly doesn't work. Policy makers who deal with recalcitrant teachers—not unlike teachers who deal with recalcitrant students, by the way—yearn for a solution that's both easy and effective. Unfortunately, when they can't have both, they often settle for easy.

Linda McNeil of Rice University points out that, paradoxically, the test-driven instruction that takes place as a result of accountability-based reforms may reinforce what the *worst* instructors have been doing. "Under a prescriptive system of curriculum, student testing, and teacher assessment," she observes, "the weakest teachers were given a system to which they could readily conform."[48]

Yet I know I've read in the newspaper about states and districts that have used what you call "heavy-handed" tactics and seem to achieve some success.

Here are four reasons you should be very careful about drawing lessons from those stories:

First, high-stakes testing and other "doing to" tactics have sometimes been tried right around the same time that other, more reliable strategies were being implemented. In Texas, for example, many observers have argued that, to the extent there has been any improvement in student performance,[49] it is "largely the result not of the tests, but of smaller class sizes, rising overall spending on education and a court-ordered equalization of resources between schools serving the rich and the poor."[50] In fact, it's entirely possible that positive results in such a scenario could have been even more impressive in the *absence* of high-stakes testing.

Second, claims of miraculous improvements often turn out to offer more hype than hope. One illustration: A closer look at the allegedly amazing progress made by San Francisco public schools in the mid-1990s revealed that thousands of students who speak very little English had been excluded from testing right around the time the city's scores started to rise.[51]

Third, we need to track results for a while. Researchers have found a predictable pattern playing itself out in state after state. When tests are first administered, the scores are distressingly low. (And the headlines read: Our schools are failing! Our students are ignorant!) After a year or two, the scores begin to rise as students and teachers get used to the test. (And the headlines read: Our schools are improving! Tougher standards are working!) Then the scores level off or begin to drop—or, if a new test is substituted for the original one, even plummet. (We've grown complacent! Even *tougher* standards are needed!) Politicians and journalists assume they are watching a rise and fall in the quality of instruction, despite the fact that this familiar cycle is largely an artifact of the testing itself.[52]

Fourth, and perhaps most important, keep in mind that claims of higher achievement are almost always based on the very test that was administered to "raise standards." As anyone with even a smattering of knowledge about educational measurement will tell you, a given test cannot be used as a lever (that is, as part of a high-stakes program that says "Make these scores go up, or else") *and* as a measure of the success of that program. You're not getting a valid picture of learning; you're getting a reflection of students having been drilled relentlessly to beat this particular test.

In thinking about claims of improvement, never forget that standardized tests in general are quite limited. Anyone who argues that an accountability program (or any new policy, for that matter) has been successful ought to be asked what exactly is meant by "successful." If, as is often the case, the claim rests upon nothing more than higher test scores, we would do well to reply, "Given what we know about these tests, you have yet to offer meaningful evidence of success." (This point is especially relevant when heavily scripted programs involving direct instruction of low-level skills are justified as "effective" solely on the basis of short-term test gains.)

Speaking of meaningful evidence, I'm wondering whether there is any research specific to the effects of high-stakes testing.

Not much. That in itself is remarkable; it means that our children are, in effect, being used as involuntary subjects in a huge high-stakes experiment.[53] But what's worse is that the limited evidence that *does* exist suggests that this approach isn't even successful on its own terms—that is, at promoting narrowly defined academic achievement. Historically speaking, high-stakes testing has "failed wherever it has been tried," according to Linda Darling-Hammond, professor at Stanford University. And in the mid-1990s, states *without* high-stakes exit exams actually showed more improvement on another standardized test, the eighth-grade National Assessment of Educational Progress (NAEP), than states with such graduation exams. Evidence from other countries is similarly discouraging.[54]

Also relevant here are small-scale studies that look at how various approaches to school reform affect individual classrooms. Researchers at the University of Colorado asked a group of fourth-grade teachers to teach a specific task. About half the teachers were told that when they were finished, their students must "perform up to standards" and do well on a test. The other teachers were simply invited to "facilitate the children's learning." The result: Students in the "standards" classrooms did not learn the task as well as those in the other group.[55]

Really? Why would teachers who had their attention focused on bringing up the scores end up with students whose scores were lower?

Ask a roomful of teachers to speculate on why that happened, and you'll get a roomful of different answers, almost all of them plausible. Here's one clue: In a similar study conducted in upstate New York, teachers in the "standards" condition were observed while they taught. Essentially, they turned into drill sergeants, removing any opportunity for the students to play an active role in their own learning. When the teachers were controlled, in other words, they responded by becoming controlling. That makes it harder for real learning to take place.[56]

Can we back up a moment here? You said a little while ago that the high-stakes approach is not even successful "on its own terms"— that is, at promoting achievement. What other terms are there?

Even if it did boost achievement, you'd have to weigh that against the other things it does.

First, it *drives good teachers and principals out of the profession.* Teachers are already beginning to tire of the pressure, the skewed priorities, and the disrespectful treatment as they are forced to implement a curriculum largely determined by test manufacturers or state legislators. Some are talking about quitting—or at least avoiding the grade levels where tests are routinely administered, such as fourth grade. The most promising teacher candidates, too, may be reluctant to begin a career that is increasingly centered on test results rather than on learning—or to work in a system that will try to manipulate them with rewards and punishments.

Similarly, it's becoming difficult to find qualified people who will agree to take a position as a principal. One middle school principal in Kentucky says he has watched his colleagues "disappear from the ranks. No one wants to blame it on [high-stakes testing programs], but from my perspective as a practicing principal, many of them made it clear they weren't going to put up with unreasonable demands."[57] Because those who are leaving include some of the best teachers and administrators, the paradoxical result, once again, is that the "tougher standards" movement has the effect of lowering standards.

Second, even if they stay, educators may become *defensive and competitive.* In a high-stakes environment, teachers and principals understandably may feel the need to prove that low scores were not their fault. Moreover, it may set them against one another:

> A state with which we are familiar adopted a program that based high school mathematics teachers' annual raises on gains in their students' achievement scores. The next year some of the top teachers in the state resigned in disgust. Those who remained entered into intense competition with one another, which disrupted school programs and caused morale to drop throughout the state. (Among other things, some math teachers demanded that their schools restrict extracurricular activities, cancel school assemblies, and abolish out-of-school trips that might interfere with their instructional efforts.) The following year the incentive program was dropped.[58]

Third, high-stakes testing has led to widespread *cheating.* Educators in state after state, pressured to raise test scores, have been caught coaching students inappropriately during tests or altering answer sheets afterward. Reports of such behavior always elicit condemnation of the individuals involved but rarely lead people to rethink the pressures attendant on high-stakes testing. Other dubious tactics, meanwhile, are likely to be ignored entirely, such as providing extensive support for students who are right on the border of being able to pass the tests and slighting everyone else. Some educators may even force low-achieving students to repeat a grade, not because this is likely to be in the students' best interest (which it almost never is) but because it's assumed that they'll do better on the exam the following year and in the meantime won't bring down the average of the current pool of test-takers.[59] Low-scoring students may also be designated as "special needs" to exempt them from the tests, thereby bolstering the school's overall standing.

Fourth, high-stakes testing may *turn teachers against students*. A superintendent in Florida observed that "when a low-performing child walks into a classroom, instead of being seen as a challenge, or an opportunity for improvement, for the first time since I've been in education, teachers are seeing [him or her] as a liability."[60] Needless to say, if educators "resent children who are likely, for one reason or another, to perform poorly, they cannot establish the nurturing relationship with those children that will enable the children to trust them."[61]

Fifth, it may contribute to *overspecialization*. In Ohio, the pressure to boost proficiency test scores has contributed to changes in how teachers of children from age nine to fourteen are certified by the state, forcing them to specialize in only two content areas, such as math and science. This means that the kind of departmentalization that has created such a fragmented educational experience in high school may now happen, thanks to testing pressures, as early as fourth grade. (Departmentalization, in turn, tends to support other problematic practices, such as the use of letter grades and the segregation of students by alleged ability.)

Sixth, it *narrows the conversation about education*. The more that scores are emphasized, the less discussion there is about the proper goals of schooling and the more educators are reduced to finding the most efficient means for what has become the de facto goal: doing better on tests. Furthermore, there is less inclination to use (or develop) alternative assessments. "As long as a school or teacher has adequate test scores, what happens in the classroom is irrelevant"; poor test scores, meanwhile, are viewed as indicators that change is needed, "no matter what happens in the classroom."[62]

Finally, there's the big one: the most predictable consequence of high-stakes testing, which is being noted with increasing bitterness by teachers all over the country but is rarely understood by those outside the classroom.

And that is . . . ?

High-stakes testing has radically altered the kind of instruction that is offered in American schools, to the point that "teaching to the test" has become a prominent part of the nation's educational landscape. Teachers often feel obliged to set aside other subjects for days, weeks, or (particularly in schools serving low-income students) even months at a time in order to devote themselves to boosting students' test scores. Indeed, both the content and the format of instruction are affected; the test essentially *becomes* the curriculum. For example, when students will be judged on the basis of a multiple-choice test, teachers may use multiple-choice exercises and in-class tests beforehand. This has aptly been called the "dumbing down" of instruction, although curiously not by the conservative critics with whom that phrase is normally associated.

More strikingly, teachers will dispense with poetry and focus on prose, breeze through the Depression and linger on the Cold War, cut back on social studies to make room for more math—all depending on what they think will be emphasized on the tests. They may even place all instruction on hold and spend time administering and reviewing practice tests. The implications for the quality of teaching are not difficult to imagine, particularly if better scores on high-stakes exams are likely to result more from memorizing math facts and algorithms, for example, than from understanding concepts. As two researchers put it, "The controlling, 'top-down' push for higher standards may actually produce a lower quality of education, precisely because its tactics constrict the means by which teachers most successfully inspire students' engagement in learning, and commitment to achieve."[63]

Teachers across the country struggle with variations of this dilemma, worrying about their jobs as well as the short-term price their students may have to pay for more authentic learning. The choices are grim: Either the teachers capitulate, or they struggle courageously to resist this, or they find another career. "Everywhere we turned," one group of educators reported, "we heard stories of teachers who were being told, in the name of 'raising standards,' that they could no longer teach reading using the best of children's literature but instead must fill their classrooms and their days with worksheets, exercises, and drills." The result in any given classroom was that "children who had been excited about books, reading with each other, and talking to each other were now struggling to categorize lists of words."[64]

Even in classes less noticeably ravaged by the imperatives of test preparation, there are hidden costs—opportunities missed, intellectual roads not taken. For one thing, teachers are less likely to work together in teams.[65] For another, within each classroom "the most engaging questions kids bring up spontaneously—'teachable moments'—become annoyances."[66] Excitement about learning pulls in one direction; covering the material that will be on the test pulls in the other. Thoughtful discussions about current events are especially likely to be discarded because what's in today's paper won't be on the exam. Furthermore, it is far more difficult for teachers to attend to children's social and moral development—holding class meetings, building a sense of community, allowing time for creative play, developing conflict-resolution skills, and so on—when the only thing that matters is scores on tests that, of course, measure none of these things. Indeed, there is anecdotal evidence that a greater emphasis on heavy-handed discipline to enforce order may be one more consequence of the imperative for test preparation.

These disturbing changes can take place whenever people's attention is drawn to test scores. But if bonuses for high scores are dangled in front of teachers or schools—or punitive "consequences" are threatened for low scores—the chances are far greater that a meaningful curriculum will be elbowed out to make room for test-oriented instruction. And this is most likely to happen in schools that serve low-income students.[67]

To talk about the kind of teaching that takes place in the

name of raising scores is to talk about the kind of teaching that is abandoned. First to be sacrificed in a school or district where rewards or punishments attend the results of such testing is a more vibrant, integrated, active, "student-centered" kind of instruction. (Arguably, the alternative to a student-centered classroom today is not one that is teacher-centered but one that is legislature-centered.) The more prominent and relevant the tests become, the more difficult it is for teachers to invite students on an intellectual adventure, to help them acquire the ability and desire to solve realistic problems in a thoughtful way. One example can stand in for thousands:

> Kathy Greeley, a Cambridge, Massachusetts, middle school teacher, had devised a remarkable unit in which every student selected an activity that he or she cared about and then proceeded to become an expert in it. Each subject, from baking to ballet, was researched intensively, described in a detailed report, and taught to the rest of the class. The idea was to hone researching and writing skills, but also to help each student feel like an expert in something and to heighten everyone's appreciation for the craft involved in activities they may not have thought much about. In short, it was the kind of academic experience that people look back on years later as a highlight of their time in school. But now her students will not have the chance: "Because we have so much content material to cover, I don't have the time to do it," she says ruefully. "I mean, I've got to do the Industrial Revolution because it's going to be on the test."

But surely not all states have tests that are as fact-based as the one that's apparently being given where this teacher lives.

Actually, the tests in most other states are worse! So if exams like the Massachusetts Comprehensive Assessment System (MCAS), which purportedly requires problem solving and higher-level understanding, have the effect of squeezing out some of the best teaching, imagine how dire the situation is in states where the tests are truly appalling.

Indeed, more and more teachers around the country feel compelled not only to teach testable facts in test-like fashion but to impart advice about test-taking, per se. This is not only an egregious waste of time but educationally harmful to the extent that students begin to generalize such strategies—for example, adopting the habit of skimming a book, looking for facts they might be asked about on a test, rather than thinking deeply about and responding to what they are reading. But if clever strategies (for example, skipping to the questions first, then going back to the passage to find the answers) *are* effective, this means that a high test score is partly just a function of good test-taking skills. If students' scores can indeed be raised by teaching them tricks or by cramming them full of carefully chosen information, this should be seen not as an endorsement of such methods but as a devastating revelation about how little we have to learn from the results of these tests.

Linda Darling-Hammond offers this analogy: Suppose it has been decided that hospital standards must be raised, so all patients must now have their temperatures taken on a regular basis. Shortly before the thermometers are inserted, doctors administer huge doses of aspirin and cold drinks. Remarkably, then, it turns out that no one is running a fever! The quality of hospital care is at an all-time high! What is really going on, of course, is completely different from providing good health care and assessing it accurately—just as teaching to the test is completely different from providing good instruction and assessing it accurately.[68]

Is that really a good analogy? Those doctors are simply cheating.

Right. And that's exactly why the analogy is apt: Teaching to the test could be described as "legal cheating." However, unlike the kind of cheating that is widely condemned (giving kids the answers) or the kind that would be condemned if it were publicized (flunking potentially low-scoring students or shuffling them off to special ed.), drilling students so they'll do well on the test even if they're not really learning much of value is generally accepted. In many areas, it is expected; indeed, it is even *demanded* by people who think that only test scores matter—or people who are bullied into acting as though they thought that was true.

Remember: If one district or school outscores another, a hefty part of that difference is probably due to socioeconomic factors and is therefore pedagogically meaningless. But even if we focus on a single district or school, in effect holding those factors constant, improvement on standardized tests over time may be worse than meaningless; it may be reason for concern. Time spent preparing students to succeed on such tests is time that could have been spent helping them become critical, creative, curious thinkers.

But do these imperatives have to be mutually exclusive?

Even for us to acknowledge that they are conceptually distinct, that they *could* lead to different practices, would represent a big improvement over the tendency to conflate the two—a tendency reflected in speeches offered by politicians, reports issued by business groups, and articles published in the popular press, all of which talk about "excellence" and "raising the bar," "tougher standards" and "higher expectations," and clearly mean nothing more than higher scores on standardized tests.

In practice, higher scores do not necessarily signal higher-quality learning. At a recent gathering of educational measurement experts (sponsored by the National Science Foundation and the RAND Corporation), agreement emerged that "in states where test scores are rising, the improvements may have nothing to do with whether schools have upgraded their teaching and curricula" but instead reflect "students' and teachers' increased familiarity with the state assessments" and "improved test-taking skills unrelated to the curriculum."[69]

But we can go further than this. Just as we've seen that high scores and deeper thinking tend to be inversely related (see p. 10), so it is that teaching geared toward higher scores and teaching geared toward higher quality learning can often pull in opposite directions. It's naïve to believe that teachers can continue providing the best kind of instruction while remaining confident that their students will do just fine on standardized tests. If a test requires coverage of a great deal of material—however superficially—then exploring a few things deeply will be poor preparation for the test even though it may be far more effective for achieving various intellectual goals. This is especially true in science and social studies, where the best way to teach (according to a growing consensus among educators in those fields) is diametrically opposed to the best way to raise test scores, which may involve textbooks, lectures, and worksheets to promote memorization of dates and definitions. The former is about discovery; the latter is about coverage. Thus, "schools that frown on teaching to tests might be singled out as 'underperforming'"[70]—penalized for doing what is best for kids.

Linda McNeil's description of the choice faced by Texas educators will be instantly and painfully familiar to teachers across the country—but may come as news to some parents, school board members, politicians, and reporters:

> The myth of the proficiencies [that is, the standards] was that because they were aimed at minimum skills, they would change only the weakest teaching. The "good" teachers would as a matter of course "already be covering" this material and so would not have to make adjustments. In fact, the transformation of the curriculum into received knowledge, to be assessed by students' selection of one answer among four provided on a computer-scored test, undermined both the quality and quantity that "good teachers" could present to their students. . . . [Thus,] teachers faced serious ethical dilemmas. They could teach to the proficiencies and assure high test scores for their students. Or they could teach the curricula they had been developing (and wanted to continue to develop) and teach not only a richer subject matter but also one that was aimed at students' understanding and their long-term learning, not the short-term goals inherent in the district testing of memorized fragments. This was not an easy choice.[71]

Incredibly, states like Texas, North Carolina, and Virginia, where the tests are among the worst and the use of rewards and punishment to mandate a curriculum centered on those tests is particularly heavy-handed, have been held up as models for other states to follow. Such is the educational climate of our times: you can't be too tough, you can't test too much, and there's no policy so ludicrous that you can't get away with it—even brag about it—as long as you remember to recite the magical words "accountability" and "tougher standards."

Again, though, even in states where the standards are less objectionable, the one-size-fits-all testing systems have approximately the same effect on quality curriculum that a noose has on breathing. Today's mail brings a report of an innovative medical mentorship program at a middle school in New

Rochelle, New York, where eighth graders follow doctors through the day and write rigorous research papers. "Like dozens of other programs statewide that use assessments other than standardized exams," this one "doesn't comply with the state's new educational standards" and is slated for extinction.[72]

Part of the problem, it should be said, takes us back to the assumptions about quantification that lie behind the push for tougher standards: To talk about what happens in schools as moving forward or backward in specifiable degrees, to make a fetish of "specific, measurable goals," is not only simplistic insofar as it fails to capture what is really going on; it is destructive insofar as it changes what is going on for the worse. Once teachers and students are compelled to focus only on what can be reduced to numbers, such as how many grammatical errors are present in a composition or how many mathematical algorithms have been committed to memory, the process of thinking has been severely compromised and the best programs and classes can't survive.

The ultimate result of this sensibility is, as critics of one state's reform efforts observed, that "what can be measured reliably and validly becomes what is important to know."[73] This is the opposite of what would seem to be the sensible way to formulate an education policy—namely, to begin by agreeing on some broad outlines for what students ought to know and be able to do, and then address the question of assessment. These days, it's just the opposite: the tail of testing is wagging the educational dog.

POOR TEACHING FOR POOR KIDS

What does all this mean for poor kids and for kids of color? Even if it's true that suburban schools are being dumbed down by the tests, what about the inner-city schools? Let's face it: They're often horrendous to begin with. Won't the tests raise standards there, at least? Don't we need to "close the gap" and pay attention to kids who have been badly served for years?

Precisely because this question is so important, we need to look behind the slogans and understand the reality of what high-stakes testing—and the whole "tougher standards" doctrine—actually means for minority students, particularly those from low-income families.

Senator Paul Wellstone of Minnesota put it very well in a speech he delivered to educators in the spring of 2000:

> Making students accountable for test scores works well on a bumper sticker and it allows many politicians to look good by saying that they will not tolerate failure. But it represents a hollow promise. Far from improving education, high stakes testing marks a major retreat from fairness, from accuracy, from quality and from equity.[74]

This is true for several reasons.

The tests may be biased. For decades, critics have complained that many standardized tests are unfair because the questions require a set of knowledge and skills more likely to be possessed by children from a privileged background. It's more than a little ironic to rely on biased tests to address educational inequities.

The discriminatory effect is even worse in the case of norm-referenced tests, where the objective is to spread out the scores as much as possible. Pretend you are charged with creating such a test. Since all students have been exposed to classroom instruction, what's a good way to ensure that not everyone will be able to answer a given question? Simple: Design it so that knowledge gained *outside* of school provides a big advantage. Naturally, such knowledge is more likely to be acquired by students whose parents are affluent and well educated, students who have attended a good preschool, own a computer, overhear thoughtful conversations about current events, are taken on interesting trips, and so on.[75]

Another factor deals with the mechanics of test design. The people who produce norm-referenced tests not only want questions that are answered correctly by only some students; they also want questions that are answered correctly by those who do well on the test overall. If a particular question contained a phrase in Spanish, for example, it's possible that many of those who got it wrong would have done well on the rest of the test, and many of those who got it right would have done poorly on the rest of the test. That's exactly what the test designers want to avoid: They want a nice, clean correspondence between the whole and the parts. What that means, though, is that "a test item on which African-Americans do particularly well but whites do not is likely to be discarded because of the interaction of two factors: African-Americans are a minority, and African Americans tend to score low."[76] Thus, in this way, too, the tests basically build in discrimination. And it's recently become clear that a test doesn't even have to be norm-referenced for this kind of bias to be present: It appears to be a part of the Texas Assessment of Academic Skills (TAAS), and possibly other state tests as well.[77]

Guess who can afford better test preparation. When the stakes rise, people seek help anywhere they can find it, and companies eager to profit from this desperation by selling test preparation materials and services have begun to appear on the scene, most recently tailoring their products to exams offered by individual states. Naturally, affluent families, schools, and districts are better able to afford such products—and the most effective versions of such products—thereby exacerbating the inequity of such testing. Moreover, when poorer schools do manage to scrape together the money to buy these materials, it's often at the expense of books and other educational resources they really need.[78]

The quality of instruction declines most for those who have least. Standardized tests, as we've seen, tend to measure the temporary acquisition of facts and skills, including the skill of test-taking itself, more than genuine understanding. To that extent, the fact that more such tests are likely to be used and emphasized in schools with higher percentages of minority students[79] predictably results in poorer-quality teaching in such schools. The use of a high-stakes strategy only underscores the preoccupation with these tests and, as a result, accelerates a reliance on direct instruction techniques and endless practice tests. "Skills-based instruction, the type to which most children of color are subjected, tends to foster low-level uniformity and subvert academic potential," as Dorothy Strickland, an African American professor at Rutgers University, has remarked.[80]

To be sure, many city schools that serve low-income children of color were second-rate to begin with. Now, however, some of these schools, in Chicago, Houston, Baltimore, and elsewhere, are arguably becoming *third*-rate as the pressures of high-stakes testing lead to a more systematic use of low-level,

drill-and-skill teaching, often in the context of packaged programs purchased by school districts. Thus, when someone
emphasizes the importance of "higher expectations" for minority children, it is vital that we reply, "Higher expectations to
do what? Bubble in more ovals correctly on a bad test—or pursue engaging projects that promote sophisticated thinking?"
The movement driven by "tougher standards," "accountability," and similar slogans actually *lowers* meaningful expectations
insofar as it relies on standardized testing as the primary measure of achievement. The more that poor children fill in worksheets on command (in an effort to raise their test scores), the
further they fall behind affluent kids who are more likely to
get lessons that help them understand ideas.[81] And if the
drilling does result in higher scores, the proper response is not
celebration but outrage: The test results may well have
improved at the expense of real learning.

It is not only understandable but entirely appropriate that
civil rights groups, attorneys, and sympathetic judges would
condemn the disparities between black and white, between rich
and poor. But when they uncritically rely on standardized tests
as indicators of how much progress has been made to close these
gaps, they may be unaware of how much harm they are doing
by legitimating and perpetuating a reliance on such testing—
a reliance that ultimately damages low-income and minority
students most of all.

Standards aren't the main ingredient that's in low supply.
Anyone who is serious about addressing the inequities of
American education would naturally want to investigate differences in available resources. A good argument could be
made that the fairest allocation strategy, which is only common sense in some countries, is to provide not merely equal
amounts across schools and districts, but more for the most
challenging student populations. This does happen in some
states—by no means all—but even when it does, the money
is commonly offered as a short-term grant (hardly sufficient
to compensate for years of inadequate funding) and often ear-
marked for test preparation rather than for higher quality
teaching. Worse, high-stakes testing systems may provide more
money to those already successful (for example, in the form
of bonuses for good scores) and less to those whose need is
greatest. Thus, the poorest families, schools, and towns suffer

most from policies enacted by officials who claim to be committed to higher standards for all students.

In any event, many of these officials, along with like-minded journalists and other observers, are apt to minimize the matter of resources and assume that everything deficient about education for poor and minority children can be remedied by more forceful demands that we "raise the bar." The implication here would seem to be that teachers and students *could* be doing a better job but have for some reason chosen not to do so and need only be bribed or threatened into improvement. (In fact, this is the tacit assumption behind all incentive systems.) The focus among policy makers has been on standards of outcome rather than standards of opportunity. This, as Senator Wellstone observed, just sets up poor kids to fail:

> People talk about using tests to motivate students to do well and using tests to ensure that we close the achievement gap. This kind of talk is backwards and unfair. We cannot close the achievement gap until we close the gap in investment between poor and rich schools. . . . [Otherwise,] we hold children responsible for our own inaction and unwillingness to live up to our own promises and our own obligations. We confuse their failure with our own. This is a harsh agenda indeed for America's children.[82]

To make matters worse, some supporters of high-stakes testing have not just ignored but contemptuously dismissed the relevance of barriers to achievement in certain neighborhoods. Explanations about very real obstacles such as racism, poverty, fear of crime, low teacher salaries, inadequate facilities, and language barriers are sometimes written off as mere "excuses." This is at once naïve and callous, and, like any other example of minimizing the relevance of structural constraints, ultimately serves the interests of those fortunate enough not to face them.

Yet some people, who may be naïve but don't seem to be callous, really think they're helping poor kids by supporting high-stakes testing. With such tests, they say, a high school diploma won't be worthless, as it is now.

If high school diplomas are worthless unless they're awarded on the basis of a standardized test score, then you and I might as well toss ours in the trash can. The only way someone could argue that such tests are necessary today but weren't necessary for us is by claiming that schools are worse than they used to be. As I've already noted, a considerable body of data exists to debunk that claim.

In any case, what a test-based diploma signifies is merely that the person who possesses it passed a test. Much of this book has been devoted to questioning the link between testing well and learning well—and, indeed, to showing that the latter may be sacrificed when the former takes precedence. The best way to improve secondary school education is to address what is deficient about it (huge schools, short periods, letter and number grades, lecture- and textbook-based instruction, and so on) as well as to provide for more meaningful kinds of assessments of what students really understand and can do with what they understand. "Pass this standardized test or you don't graduate" not only fails to address these problems; it actively discourages people from addressing them because now all eyes are on the test.

Even if it were true that diplomas these days are meaningless, and that schools are handing them out to legions of unqualified ignoramuses, it's hard to see how it makes sense to punish the students by refusing to let them graduate for what are clearly problems with the system.[83]

And that leads to the final observation about high-stakes testing and equity:

Those allegedly being helped will be driven out. When rewards and punishments are applied to educators, those who teach low-scoring populations are the most likely to be branded as failures and may decide to leave the profession. Even those who stay, as noted earlier, may come to see low-scoring students as a liability, something that stands between them and a bonus. In either case, we would expect minority and low-income students to be particularly affected by the incessant pressure on teachers to raise scores.

But that's not even the worst of it. When high stakes are applied to the students themselves, there is little doubt about who will be disproportionately denied diplomas as a consequence of failing an exit exam—or will simply give up and drop out in anticipation of such an outcome. If states persist in making a student's fate rest on a single test, the likely result over the next few years will be nothing short of catastrophic.

Unless we act to stop this, we will be facing a scenario that might be described without exaggeration as an educational ethnic cleansing.

IF NOT STANDARDIZED TESTS, THEN WHAT?

Obviously we need some way to ensure that poor kids—in fact, all kids—are getting a decent education. So aren't we pretty much stuck with standardized tests, however flawed they might be?

Absolutely not. The only thing at which standardized tests are uniquely efficient is ranking one school, or state, against another. Once we understand how pointless such comparisons are, how they are less about excellence than about victory, we may come to question the demand for such tests. They aren't necessary—or even particularly useful—for determining how good a given school is, or how effectively a given student has learned.

It's important to remember that those two goals are different: A method for helping us learn about individual student achievement may not be the best way to monitor the performance of entire schools or districts, and vice versa. So let's start with the question: How can parents be confident that their child is learning?

To begin with, they can be given written descriptions ("narratives") from the teacher—or, better yet, they can participate in conversations *with* the teacher. What teachers are reporting is, in turn, based on continuous observations of children and their activities. The most skillful educators tend not to rely very much on pencil-and-paper tests, even of their own devising.[84] Instead, everything from the kinds of tasks that have been assigned to the way the classroom has been organized is intended to help the teacher know as much as possible about how students are making sense of things. Parents shouldn't be worried about a teacher who rarely gives tests; they should be worried about one who needs to give a lot of tests because he or she may lack a feel for how kids' minds work.

Parents can also learn a great deal about their children's accomplishments—what they're capable of doing and where they may be falling short—when teachers use "performance assessments." These are opportunities for students to demonstrate their proficiency by actually *doing* something: designing and conducting (and explaining the results of) an experiment, speaking in a foreign language, writing a play, and so on. Ideally, the students themselves help to decide the best medium for showing what they can do. Ted Sizer and the Coalition of Essential Schools, for example, have provided guidelines for "exhibitions": projects that reflect evidence of sustained thought and proficiency across the disciplines.[85]

One especially intriguing version of a performance assessment is called a "portfolio," modeled on what adults in some fields, notably the arts, compile to document their professional accomplishments. Here, students collect what they've done over a period of time, not just because it's helpful to have all that material in one place but because the process of choosing what to include—and deciding how to evaluate it—becomes an opportunity for them to reflect on their past learning as well as to set new goals. The portfolio's contents may be selected to demonstrate improvement over time, or to reflect how many different kinds of projects have been attempted. Students might share their portfolios with the rest of the class, or consult with their peers on what should go into them. Like other forms of performance assessment, they provide data far more meaningful than what could be learned from a conventional test, standardized or otherwise, about what students can do and where they still need help.

But wouldn't parents then be dependent on the teacher's interpretation and evaluation of those assessments?

To some extent, yes, but parents also should be able to see for themselves what the child has done. They can watch a student's formal presentation of her project. In some schools, moreover, parent-teacher conferences are attended by students—indeed, *directed* by students, who decide how to share information about their accomplishments.[86] Remarkable conversations can occur at such an occasion, as the student walks his parents through the portfolio, responding to questions about its contents (Why did you decide to include this? How did you manage to do that? What's the difference between these two items?).

The teacher does play an integral role in this process, not only in providing structure and guidance to the student but also in helping the parent make sense of how successful the child has been. After all, we turn to physicians and attorneys for their expert evaluations. Why shouldn't we expect education professionals to play a similar role? This question isn't merely rhetorical because, sadly, some parents have a tendency to discount the teacher's evaluation, mesmerized as they are by the results of standardized tests, which are falsely believed to be objective.

Worse, even some teachers have come to trust test scores more than their own judgment. It's not unusual to hear of parents who ask a teacher about problems their child is having in school, only to have the teacher immediately walk over to the closet and fish out the student's last set of test results. Somewhere along the way such teachers have been led to discount their own impressions of students, formed and reformed through months of up-close observations and interactions. Instead, they defer to the results of a one-shot, high-pressure, machine-scored exam, attributing almost magical properties to the official numbers.

But how is a parent supposed to know that the teacher's own assessment is credible?

We could just as well ask why some parents assume from the start (without evidence) that it *isn't* credible, while assuming (contrary to the available evidence) that the test *is* credible.

Having said that, I would agree that it's often reasonable to want some kind of corroborative evidence about how well one's child is doing. But it's important to realize that standardized tests aren't the only way, or the best way, to provide it. What makes more sense is a system that begins with the teacher's appraisal, basing assessment on an analysis of multiple examples of students' learning by the person closest to it, but then uses outside evaluators to validate the teacher's judgment and enhance parents' confidence in it.[87]

At least two systems exist to provide this kind of reassurance: the Learning Record and Work Sampling. Both are based on a bottom-up rather than top-down approach, using an established format to help teachers document each student's learning by sampling different things she has done, thereby allowing the teacher to analyze a pattern of performance observed and documented over time in natural settings.[88]

Don't these alternative forms of assessment take more time?

Compared to dashing off a letter grade? Yes. Compared to drilling kids on standardized test materials and format? Maybe not. In any case, much of the authentic assessment process is integrated into the learning that kids are doing as opposed to something that comes afterward.

But do you really think this kind of assessment system will satisfy parents? An awful lot of them seem to want standardized test scores.

The good news is that this preference is rarely an informed one. Few parents have ever been invited to consider the weaknesses of these tests or the fact that alternatives exist. They have been served a steady diet of test scores from newspapers, politicians, and top school officials—and have been encouraged to believe this is the logical way to monitor how their children are doing. That suggests the possibility that parents may be open to other options. And indeed, the more information about standardized tests they acquire, the more dubious the tests are likely to seem; similarly, the more they learn about performance assessments, the more interested parents are likely to become.

You're sure this isn't just wishful thinking?

Well, in the 1999 Phi Delta Kappa/Gallup poll of the general public, respondents were asked which of four methods "would provide the most accurate picture of a public school student's academic progress." Only 27 percent picked standardized test scores; most chose a classroom-based approach to assessment. "Examples of the student's work" was the top choice (33 percent), and the balance was divided between letter grades and written observations by the teacher.[89] Subsequent surveys have found similar results.[90]

Thus, public support for conventional tests may be thin to begin with. And once people are offered more details about other forms of assessment, the results are even more dramatic. One example: a survey of parents of third graders in an ethnically diverse, working-class district near Denver found higher levels of support for performance assessments than for standardized tests once the former option was presented and explained. When parents were shown examples of standardized test questions ("How much change will you get if you have $6.55 and spend $4.32? [a] $2.23 [b] $2.43 [c] $3.23 [d] $10.87") as well as performance assessment questions ("Suppose you couldn't remember what 8 x 7 is. How could you figure it out?"), "by far the majority of respondents preferred performance assessments." Many remarked that the latter were more challenging and gave teachers more insight into what the students understood and where they were struggling. The researchers admitted being "surprised that parents rated informal sources of information—talking to the teacher and seeing graded samples of their child's work—as more useful than standardized tests for learning about their 'child's progress in school' and even for judging the 'quality of education provided at their child's school.' " Clearly, they concluded, "parents' favorable ratings of standardized national tests do not imply a preference for such measures over other less formal sources of information."[91]

Educating parents about alternatives may take a while, though. What do we do in the meantime, while standardized tests are still widely used?

We do everything possible to minimize the intrusiveness and harm of those tests. That includes revisiting the criteria described on pages 11–17: Tests should not be timed. They should not be given to young children. They should not be given too frequently. They should not be norm-referenced—or reported in such a way as to emphasize rankings rather than absolute scores. They should not consist of multiple-choice questions. They should be designed to tap students' understanding of ideas rather than their ability to memorize lists of facts and definitions.

And what if our goal isn't to see how our own kids are doing but to assess an entire school or district? Aren't people demanding accountability in the form of standardized test results?

First, let's look more closely at those alleged demands. Some of the very people who shrug their shoulders and insist that "the public" wants tests are in fact feeding that fervor: the politicians and pundits who attack public schooling, using misleading claims to stir up discontent; the legislators who subject children to more and more tests; the newspapers that publish charts ranking schools (and articles evaluating schools) primarily on the basis of test scores; and even real estate agents who sell neighborhoods on that same basis. Of course, there is some truth to the claim that parents and other taxpayers want accountability and expect to see schools rated by their scores. But that truth is partial and self-serving, just as it is when producers of graphically violent movies and video games argue that they're just responding to what people want. Public officials, journalists, and others could be helping to educate the public about alternatives—or about the deficiencies of standardized tests—instead of contributing to a general expectation that we need more of the same.

Keep in mind that only recently have we heard calls for "holding schools accountable" that are quite this frequent and quite this shrill. We tend to suffer from a kind of collective amnesia, assuming that whatever is happening at the moment is unavoidable. More to the point, endorsing the idea of accountability is quite different from holding students and teachers accountable specifically for raising test scores. We need to help people see that the first doesn't entail the second—and, indeed, that genuine accountability and authentic standards are *undermined* by a myopic emphasis on testing. Remember that the Denver area study (p. 45) found that parents who learned about performance measures ended up preferring them not only for assessing their own children but also for assessing the quality of schools.

You said that for as long as we're using standardized tests to assess students, we should at least make sure they're not timed, not multiple-choice, and so on. What about while we're using these tests to assess schools or districts?

The same recommendations apply, and we should pay special attention to the fact that, just as students shouldn't be compared to one another, so norm-referenced testing doesn't make sense for schools, districts, or states. What matters is how each one is doing in absolute terms—that is, with reference to a given standard of achievement—not whether it's doing better than others. Also, results should always be evaluated in light of the special challenges faced by a given school or district: A large number of students with special needs, or a very low-income community, provides a necessary context in which to understand a set of results.

We should also keep in mind that if we're assessing whole schools or districts, there is really no reason to test every student—just as monitoring public opinion doesn't require that pollsters talk to every voter in the country. It makes sense to test a cross-section of the relevant population of students. One sampling technique consists of giving each batch of students a different part of a larger test. When the results are combined, a picture emerges of how well the whole group did. (However, even if all students *are* given the entire test—which is, of course, a lot more expensive—it's unnecessary and probably unwise to release individual scores.)

Again, though, the point to be emphasized is that we don't need to accept a major role for standardized testing at all. At most, it should be "an *occasional adjunct,* used for obtaining certain basic but limited information"[92]—which is to say, only one part of a much broader picture of student achievement.

So what else do we use to paint that broader picture?

The best way to judge schools is by visiting them and looking for evidence of learning and interest in learning. In another publication I've offered a set of indicators—a list of good signs and possible reasons to worry[93]—but thoughtful observation is what matters even if different criteria are applied.

Parents can also observe what happens at home. If their kids often chatter excitedly about something they figured out in class, if they not only can read but do read (on their own), if they persist in playing with ideas and come to think carefully and deeply about things, then this probably speaks well for the school they attend. It's not that these behaviors correlate with evidence of school success; these behaviors *are* the evidence of school success.

Is it hard to quantify such things? Yes. That suggests a limit not of these indicators, but of quantification itself. Many people who say we need some way of evaluating schools really mean we need some way of reducing schools to numbers, which is not the same thing. To reject the most meaningful criteria because they are qualitative is to put "the quest for accurate measurement—and control—above the quest for educationally and morally defensible policies."[94]

And for those who insist on something more systematic or standardized?

Even then, we have to remember that learning takes place in classrooms, not in districts or states. To get a sense of how our schools are doing, we have to start where the learning is and move out from there. That can be done by using the same kind of classroom performance assessments described earlier and relying on outside readers or validated rating scales to increase confidence in the teachers' judgments about students' learning. To sample the projects of a number of students (and the evaluations of those projects) is to get a sense of the quality of the school as a whole.

One example: The Central Park East Secondary School in New York City brings in external reviewers—experts who don't teach at the school—to look at, talk about, and rate a sample of what students have done through the year "in order to provide all concerned parties with a 'second' look at our criteria and standards. This is for the purpose solely of assessing the school's standards, not the individual's right to a diploma."[95]

 Each school should be encouraged to develop its own criteria for self-evaluation, inviting students, teachers, parents, and others in the community to decide what will help them determine how effectively they've been meeting their goals and what improvements can be made.[96] How can we provide useful feedback to educators and to students? What are the earmarks of a truly inspiring school? On what basis should we determine that a student is ready to graduate? You and I may disagree about the best answers to these questions, but the "tougher standards" and accountability movement is distinguished primarily by its intolerance for disagreement. Even putting aside the substantive problems with standardized testing, its use isn't offered as one of many forms of assessment. Rather, it is assumed that a single form is right for all schools, and that the state ought to be *imposing* its preferred answer on the rest of us with the force of law.

Some of those who measure learning differently also contend that if the assessment is authentic enough, it's perfectly acceptable to teach to the test—or even to attach high stakes to the test—because then we'd be mandating better-quality instruction. Don't they have a point there? Wouldn't you agree that everything depends on the quality of the assessment?

A lot depends on it, but not everything. As Edward Haertel at Stanford University argues, "The fundamental deficiency of high-stakes testing as an education policy tool lies in the logic of the reform strategy itself, not in the reliance on one format of test item versus another."[97] Here's why:

1. It's objectionable to use assessments—any assessments—as levers to *make* teachers change what they're doing in order to be rewarded or avoid being punished. This is another example of doing things *to* people rather than working *with* them to bring about improvement. No matter how laudable the new standards for teaching, they cannot be shoved down teachers' throats. Rather, teachers have to want to change what they're doing. "We don't need or want teachers to simply accept the new gospel . . . just because some authority figures say it is a good idea or because we're going to scare them with an external test."[98]

2. Attitudes aside, educators need help to be able to teach in a way that promotes creative and critical thinking. Pressure in the form of better tests isn't sufficient even if it were desirable.[99]

3. When disproportionate attention is focused on results— that is, on *how well* students are performing—this tends to distract them from attending to *what* they're learning.[100] In the words of two leading educational psychologists, Martin Maehr and Carol Midgley, "An overemphasis on assessment can actu-

ally undermine the pursuit of excellence."[101] That's true regardless of the quality of the assessment.

4. Attempts to hold teachers accountable for improving scores on more ambitious tests will likely lead them to second-guess these new measures and try to drill students on their specific formats and contents. "Teachers can narrow instruction to the type of performance demanded by a performance-based assessment just as they can teach to a multiple-choice test."[102] This is disturbing if only because no assessment can cover all of what we want students to know and be able to do. Therefore, to teach to even good external tests is to teach only a part of what should be taught.[103] Moreover, the validity of the assessment may be compromised if teachers are explicitly trying to teach to it.

FIGHTING THE TESTS

All right, let's say I'm persuaded that standardized tests are bad news. Trouble is, they're so incredibly pervasive that I wonder whether there's really anything we can do about them.

Far more discouraging than hearing someone defend the standards-and-testing movement is hearing someone who agrees the tests are destructive and unnecessary and then adds with a shrug, "But like it or not, we're just going to have to learn to live with them."

Real children in real classrooms suffer from that kind of defeatism. Is testing "here to stay"? If that assertion is true, it's only by virtue of its status as a self-fulfilling prophecy: Assume something is inevitable and it becomes so precisely because we've decided not to challenge it. The fact of the matter is that standardized tests are not like the weather, something to which we must resign ourselves. They haven't always existed and they don't exist in most parts of the world. What we're facing is not a force of nature but a force of politics, and political decisions can be questioned, challenged, and ultimately reversed.

Equally disturbing is a blasé kind of fatalism that says, in effect, "This too shall pass." Education has its fads, and standards on steroids may be one of them, but there is no guarantee that it will fade away on its own. Too much is invested by now; too many powerful interest groups are backing high-stakes testing for us to assume it will simply fall of its own weight. In any case, too many children will be sacrificed in the meantime if we don't take action to expedite its demise.

Whenever something in our schools is amiss—when children are set against one another in competitions, bribed or threatened into mindless obedience, drilled mercilessly on forgettable facts and isolated skills, and so forth—it makes sense for us to work on two tracks at once. We must do our best in the short term to protect students from the worst effects of a given policy, but we must also work to change or eliminate that policy. If we overlook the former—the need to minimize the harm of what is currently taking place, to devise effective coping strategies—then we do a disservice to children in the here and now. But (and this is by far the more common error) if we overlook the latter—the need to *change* the current reality—then we are condemning our children's children to having to make the best of the same unacceptable situation because it will still be around.

OK, let's start with the short-term response. Say I'm a teacher whose students are facing the prospect of tests that I don't especially like. What do I do?

You do what is necessary to prepare kids for the tests and then you get back to the real learning. Never forget the difference between these two objectives. Be clear about it in your own mind, and whenever possible, help others to understand that they're distinct. For example, you might send a letter to parents explaining what you're doing and why. ("Before we can design rigorous and exciting experiments in class, which I hope will have the effect of helping your child learn to think like a scientist, we're going to have to spend some time memorizing facts for the standardized tests being given next month. Hopefully we'll be able to return before too long to what research suggests is a more effective kind of instruction.") If you're lucky, parents might call you, indignantly demanding to know why their kids aren't able to pursue the more effective kind of instruction all the time. "Excellent question!" you'll reply, as you hand over a sheet containing the addresses and phone numbers of the local school board, state board of education, legislators, and the governor.

The first consideration to be kept in mind with respect to test preparation is to do no more than necessary. Some have argued that a relatively short period of introducing students to the content and format of the tests is sufficient to produce scores equivalent to those obtained by students who have spent the entire year in a test-prep curriculum. "You don't need to study only the test and distort your entire curriculum eight hours a day, one hundred eighty days a year, for twelve years," says Harvey Daniels, who specializes in literacy education. "We've got very interesting studies where teachers do thirty-five or thirty-eight weeks of what they think is best for kids, and then they'll give them three weeks of test cramming just before the test. And the kids do just as well as kids who have forty weeks of test-driven curriculum."[104] This is corroborated by some research that found a one-hour intensive reading readiness tutorial for young children produced test results equivalent to two *years* of skills-oriented direct instruction.[105] (Of course, this will vary depending on the child and the nature of the test.)

> One first-grade teacher in Kentucky helped her students develop their own reading program, which moves them faster and more effectively through (and beyond) the district's reading program objectives than the basal. Even so, she is required by her school's administration to put her class through a basal reader program on a prescribed weekly schedule. The solution, quickly evolved by the class: They do each week's work in the basal on Monday, with little effort, then work on the meaningful curriculum—theirs—Tuesday through Friday.[106]

The second consideration regarding test preparation is the obligation to make it as creative and worthwhile as possible. Avoid traditional drilling whenever you can. Several educators have figured out how to turn some of these tests into a kind of puzzle that children can play an active role in solving. The idea is to help students become adept at the particular skill called test-taking so they will be able to show what they already know.[107]

Finally, don't let those who are turning schools into giant test-prep centers make you into their accomplice. Don't do their dirty work for them. Indeed, whatever your position on the food chain of American education, one of your primary obligations is to be a buffer—to absorb as much pressure as possible from those above you without passing it on to those below. If you are a superintendent or assistant superintendent facing school board members who want to see higher test scores, the most constructive thing you can do is protect principals from these ill-conceived demands to the best of your ability (without losing your job in the process). If you are a building administrator, on the receiving end of test-related missives from the central office, your challenge is to shield teachers from this pressure—and, indeed, to help them pursue meaningful learning in their classrooms. If you are a teacher unlucky enough to work for an administrator who hasn't read this paragraph, your job is to minimize the impact on students. Try to educate those above you whenever it seems possible to do so, but cushion those below you every day. Otherwise you become part of the problem.

But when there are high stakes attached to the tests, how much pressure can an individual absorb? When the tests are geared to memorization, how much room is there for creative test prep?

There are limits; you're absolutely right. In some places, "the margins, those claimed spaces where even in highly prescriptive school settings [teachers] have always been able to 'really teach,' are shrinking as the accountability system becomes increasingly aligned."[108] That's why the suggestions offered above are only stopgap measures. That's why our primary focus must involve political activity, joining others to oppose the tests rather than accommodating ourselves to them.

A lot of educators, though, are reluctant to introduce politics into the schools, aren't they?

Too late! When seven-year-olds can't read good books because they are being drilled on what Jonathan Kozol calls "those obsessively enumerated particles of amputated skill associated with upcoming state exams,"[109] the schools have already been politicized. The only question is whether we'll get involved on the other side—that is, on the side of real learning. In partic-

ular, much depends on whether those teachers and administrators who already harbor (and privately acknowledge) concerns about testing are willing to go public, to take a stand, to
say, "This is bad for kids." To paraphrase a famous quotation,
all that is necessary for the triumph of damaging educational
policies is that good educators keep silent.

So where do we start? This book has described a number of
problematic beliefs and practices, and it has mentioned others
in passing. Notice that some of the pertinent issues transcend
testing. They deal with the whole "tougher standards" mindset
that underlies the tests: a confusion of harder with better, a failure to understand that too great an emphasis on how well students are doing can undermine their engagement with what
they're doing, and so on.[110] Which issue you choose to target
will depend partly on what you feel most strongly about and
partly on what is most relevant in your school, district, and state.

Your choice may also be affected by political considerations
such as where you can have the greatest impact. Those of us
who see little benefit at all from standardized tests in their current forms need to remember that this is not an all-or-noth-
ing crusade but a movement that may proceed incrementally.
One way to begin is by fighting for the principles most likely
to generate widespread support.

For example, even *Education Week*, known for its relent-
less advocacy of the standards-and-testing agenda, has
acknowledged that there is "virtually unanimous agreement
among experts that *no single measure should decide a student's
academic fate.*"[111] This is true: The prestigious National
Research Council came to that conclusion,[112] as have most
other professional organizations (such as the American Educational Research Association and the American Psychological Association), the generally pro-testing American
Federation of Teachers, and even the companies that manufacture and sell the tests. To make students repeat a grade
or deny them diplomas on the basis of a single exam is
unconscionable—yet about half the states, at this writing,
are either doing so or planning to do so. This issue is not a
bad point of entry for potential activists. It may be persua-
sive even to politicians who haven't thought much about
these issues and otherwise accept the slogans of standards
and accountability.[113]

54

Similarly, even people who are unwilling to dispense with standardized testing altogether may be open to persuasion that these tests:

• should not be the only means by which students or schools are evaluated, inasmuch as they miss (or misrepresent) many aspects of student learning that ought to be assessed some other way;

• should not, in any case, be imposed by fiat on all schools in the state, with the result that communities are prevented from making their own decisions;[114]

• should not be administered too often;

• are inappropriate for young children; and

• should be used only to rate, never to rank (since the goal is to derive useful information, not to create winners and losers and thereby discourage schools from working together).

This is not to say that we can't also be inviting people to question ideological assumptions that are harder to dislodge—to consider, for example, that a preoccupation with results can interfere with learning, or that educational progress need not (and, to some extent, *cannot*) be quantified. But even someone who resists those ideas may agree that it's wrong to make a student's future hinge on a standardized test.

How exactly do we raise those questions and make our views known?

I'm glad you asked. Some of the ideas that follow can be pursued individually, but most depend on working with others. Thus, the first suggestion is to *organize*. Find people in your area who share your concerns so you can have a more powerful impact together. Trust me, you're not alone in opposing standardized testing, but without collective action, you might as well be alone. So work with friends, neighbors, and colleagues to set up study groups, committees, phone trees, websites, and listservs. Give yourselves an organizational name, print up some letterhead; you instantly gain more credibility. (Now you're not just a bunch of rebellious teachers. You're the "[name of area] Educators Opposing Excessive Testing.") Every person who seems interested in becoming involved should be asked to find ten more potential recruits, and each of those recruits should be asked to do the same. Even as you engage in the activities listed below, you should be continuing to fold others into the effort.[115]

There's no reason, however, to waste time duplicating someone else's efforts. You may want to begin by checking out and joining an existing network if one is already active in your area. For one source of information, go to www.alfiekohn.org and click on "Standards and Testing" and then follow the links. Among other things, you'll find a collection of resources and a list of state coordinators. Some states don't have coordinators, in which case you might consider volunteering. Some states have coordinators who desperately need your help.

Of course, plenty of anti-testing efforts are taking place independent of this particular network, including active and remarkably effective parent groups in some states. Moreover, the nation's leading organization challenging standardized testing, FairTest (342 Broadway, Cambridge, MA 02139, (617)864-4810, www.fairtest.org), has a quarterly newsletter, a storehouse of useful documents, and a listserv called the Assessment Reform Network (ARN). Take advantage of /all this group has to offer, and, while you're at it, consider giving them some money.

Whether you work alone, with an existing organization, or in a new network that you help to form, begin by learning all you can about the tests used in your state as well as more generic testing issues. Then:

1. Talk to friends and neighbors at every opportunity: in line at the supermarket; in the dentist's waiting room; on airplanes; at the hairdresser's and the playground; at dinner parties and children's birthday parties. Help people in your community understand that if a local official boasts about rising test scores, they should consider responding, "You know, if that's what you're mostly concerned about, then I'm worried about the quality of my child's schooling."

2. Get in the habit of attending—and speaking out at—school board meetings and other events dealing with educational policy.

3. Let parents know they can write a letter to school administrators or board members expressing concern that test preparation is eclipsing more important learning activities. Here's a sample, provided by educational measurement specialist James Popham:[116]

Dear _____:

I want to register my concern that there seems to be an excessive emphasis in our school on getting students ready for the standardized achievement tests scheduled for administration during *(give the month of the upcoming test-administration)*. The reason I'm concerned is that I'm fearful the teaching staff's preoccupation with raising scores on those tests may be preventing the teachers from covering other important skills and knowledge that the school's students need.

I realize that you and your teaching staff are under considerable pressure to "raise test scores" because it is widely believed that students' scores on standardized achievement tests reflect the quality of a teaching staff and, by implication, the quality of the school's principal.

I've been doing some reading on that topic, and I understand why it is that students' standardized test scores do *not* provide an appropriate indication of a teaching staff's competence. Scores on those tests are more a reflection of the student population served by a school than an indication of the skill of the school's educators.

I hope that you and your staff will address this test-preparation issue in the near future. Parents want the school's children to get the very best education possible. I'm sure you do too. That will not happen, however, if our school's heavy emphasis on test-preparation deflects the school's teachers from dealing with the curricular content our children need.

Sincerely,

[Your Name]

4. Write to—or, better yet, get together a delegation of concerned citizens and then visit—your state legislators and other public officials. (This is the sort of familiar and predictable recommendation that you may be tempted to skip over, but it really ought to be taken seriously. Politicians respond to pointed and persistent lobbying, and, as a rule, they haven't heard nearly enough from those of us who feel strongly about this issue.) Your goal may be simply to educate policy makers about the effects of testing, or it may be to encourage them to oppose (or support) specific policies and legislation.

5. Write letters to the editor—or, better yet, op-eds—for your local newspaper (some samples are available at www.alfiekohn.org and www.fairtest.org).

6. Organize a delegation of educators and/or parents and request a meeting with the education reporter and top editors of your paper. Help them to see how problematic it is to cite rising or falling test scores as an indication of educational quality. Explain to them that most experts in the field oppose high-stakes testing in particular. And tell them: "Every time you publish a chart that ranks schools on the basis of test scores, our kids' learning suffers. Here's why . . ."

7. Sponsor a forum or teach-in on testing. Invite the media. Sign up new volunteers. Such a meeting might carry a provocative title to attract those already on your side (e.g., "Standardized Testing: Waste of Time or Menace to Children?"), but then again it might be promoted in more neutral terms ("Rethinking Standardized Testing") to attract more people. Those responsible for the tests can be invited to appear and respond to questions.

8. Print up bumper stickers with slogans such as STANDARD-IZED TESTING IS DUMBING DOWN OUR SCHOOLS. (Here, it is definitely appropriate to be provocative.)[117]

9. Participate in—and ensure press coverage of—some form of protest. This can include marches and demonstrations, as well as other, more targeted activities, such as those already taking place in some areas, described below.

10. Remind sympathetic school officials that under no circumstances should they brag about high (or rising) scores. To do so is not only misleading; it serves to legitimate the tests. In fact, people associated with high-scoring schools or districts have a unique opportunity to make an impact. It's easy for critics to be dismissed with a "sour grapes" argument: You're just opposed to standardized testing because it makes you look bad. But administrators and school board members in high-scoring areas can say, "Actually our students happen to do well on these stupid tests, but that's nothing to be proud of. We value great teaching and learning, which is what suffers when people become preoccupied with scores. Please join us in phasing them out."

11. Speak to educational service agencies, universities, and administrators who offer events for teachers that provide advice on raising test scores and teaching to the standards. Remind them that for every workshop or in-service event with this goal, three should be offered that encourage teachers to *challenge* the standards and tests—or at least help them think about how to protect their students from the damaging effects.

12. Invite researchers in the area to commission a survey. When it's completed, release the results at a press conference. One group of investigators suggested including these questions:

> Do the tests improve students' motivation? Do parents understand the results? Do teachers think that the tests measure the curriculum fairly? Do administrators use the results wisely? How much money is spent on assessment and related services? How much time do teachers spend preparing students for various tests? Do the media report the data accurately and thoroughly? Our surveys suggest that many districts will be shocked to discover the degree of dissatisfaction among stakeholders.[118]

13. Challenge politicians, corporate executives, and others who talk piously about the need to "raise the bar," impose "tougher standards," and ensure "accountability," to take the tests themselves. This is especially important in the case of high-stakes exit exams, which are increasingly being used to deny diplomas to students who don't pass them.

There are two ways to issue such an invitation to decision makers: first, as a private opportunity for them to learn more about (and, perhaps, understand the absurdity of) the exam; second, as a public challenge for them to take the test and agree to have their scores published in the newspaper. The first approach was used in West Bend, Wisconsin, where about thirty business leaders took a short version of the state's proposed graduation exam. They "had so much trouble with it that some wonder[ed] whether it truly will measure the quality of future employees." One bank executive—presumably a supporter of testing in the abstract until he encountered the actual test—remarked, "I think it's good to challenge students, but not like this."[119]

The second approach was taken by the *St. Petersburg Times* when it "challenged several top elected officials to join 735,000 Florida schoolchildren . . . by taking the rigorous Florida Comprehensive Assessment Test. They declined. Some did so with a sense of humor. Some admitted the math might give them fits. Others were unamused by the entire exercise. All said no."[120] Educators and parents might consider holding a press conference to issue such a public challenge, arguing that if officials fear they won't be able to pass the test, they should be prepared to justify requiring teenagers to do something that they, themselves, cannot. And if they refuse the challenge, they should be called on to defend their refusal.

14. Consider filing a lawsuit against the tests, which are potentially vulnerable in many ways. They may be inherently discriminatory. They may be used despite the absence of evidence that they are statistically valid measurement instruments. They may be inconsistent with the state's own standards—or require students to know that which hasn't yet been taught.

15. Investigate whether your state has an "opt-out" clause that allows parents to exempt their children from testing just by notifying the authorities. These are not widely known—indeed, even some activists are not always aware of their existence in their own states—but they ought to be publicized if they are on the books where you live.

16. Perhaps the most extreme—but, in the opinion of a grow-

ing number of people, well justified—strategy is to boycott the tests even where there is no opt-out provision.

That seems kind of drastic.

✳Desperate circumstances call for drastic action. The evidence offered in this book, which corroborates what many teachers already know, supports the conclusion that we are facing an educational emergency in this country. The intellectual life is being squeezed out of schools—or at least prevented from developing in schools—as tests take over the curriculum. Punitive consequences are being meted out on the basis of manifestly inadequate and inappropriate exams. Children are literally becoming sick with fear over their scores. Massive numbers of students—particularly low-income and minority students—may be pushed out of school altogether.

In short, more and more people believe that writing letters to the editor isn't enough, that a line has been crossed such that we can no longer justify our participation in—and tacit support of—these testing programs. One kind of boycott involves students who, on their own or at their parents' behest, refuse to show up for tests and make it clear why they are doing so. There are various ways in which educators can support such an action: by making sure that students and parents know that boycotts already are taking place elsewhere; by speaking out in support of those who decide to do this; by teaching students about the theory and practice of civil disobedience; by suggesting alternative educational activities in which prospective boycotters can participate on test day; and by lobbying local officials to make sure that these students are not punished. (Of course, teachers who are also parents can invite their own children to consider being part of such a protest.)

In another kind of boycott, educators themselves refuse to be part of the testing program. Like Bartleby in Melville's short story, who created an uproar when, "in a singularly mild, firm voice, replied, 'I would prefer not to,'" they declare that they simply cannot in good conscience break the shrink-wrap on those exams and thereby become part of something they believe is bad for children. It takes considerable courage for teachers to consider doing this because their jobs may be on the line. Yet that courage has already been displayed, with striking results, in other countries. "Elementary [school] achievement is high" in Japan, for example, partly because teachers in that country "are free from the pressure to teach to standardized tests." It's important to understand why there are no such tests in that country (with the exception of an infamous university admission exam): It is because Japanese teachers collectively refused to administer them. For many years now, they have successfully prevented the government from doing to their children what our government is doing to our children.[121] Similarly, in the early 1990s, teachers in England and Wales basically stopped the new national testing program in its tracks, at least for a while, by a similar act of civil disobedience. What began there "as an unfocused mishmash of voices became a united boycott involving all teacher unions, a large number of governing bodies, and mass parental support." Teachers made it clear that their action was taken in behalf of students, based on their understanding that "to teach well for the tests was in effect to teach badly."[122]

In 1999, Jim Bougas, a middle school teacher in a small town in Massachusetts, noticed that the history portion of the state's MCAS exam required students to answer questions about the Civil War even though the state's own guidelines called for that topic to be covered at the end of the year, after the test was administered. For him, this was the last straw with respect to a testing system that was already geared toward memorization and was forcing instruction to become more superficial. The teacher, a soft-spoken man who had been teaching for twenty-eight years, informed his principal that he would not administer the test. He was reassigned to the library during that period, and a stern letter of reprimand was placed in his file along with a warning not to repeat his protest. The next year, following a denial of his request to be reassigned to other duties when the test was to be administered, he agonized about what to do. Finally, he decided that if the test was just as unfair and destructive in 2000 as it had been in 1999, his response could not be any different—even at the risk of suspension or dismissal. Besides, as he told a reporter, "if the MCAS continues, I have no job because they've taken it away from me as long as I have to spend my time teaching to the test. I can't do that anymore. So I have nothing to lose."[123]

Such a protest is not only inspirational to many of us but an invitation to ponder the infinitely greater impact of *collective* action. Imagine, for example, that a teacher at any given school in your area—you, for example—quietly approached each person on the staff in turn and asked: "If ___ percent of the teachers at this school pledged to boycott the next round of testing, would you join them?" (The specific percentage would depend on what seemed realistic and yet signified sufficient participation to offer some protection for those involved.) Then, if the designated number was reached, each teacher would be invited to take part in what would be a powerful act of civil disobedience. Press coverage would likely be substantial, and despairing-but-cowed teachers in other schools might be encouraged to follow suit.

It still sounds pretty risky to me.

No question about it. Theoretically, even an entire school faculty could be fired. But the more who participate, and the more careful they are about soliciting support from parents and other members of the community beforehand, the more difficult it would be for administrators to respond harshly. (Remember, too, that some administrators are as frustrated with the testing as teachers are.) Of course, participants would have to be politically savvy, building alliances and offering a coherent, quotable rationale for their action. They would need to make it clear—at a press conference and in other forums—that they were taking this action (at considerable risk) not because they are unwilling to do more work or are afraid of being held accountable, but because these tests lower the quality of learning and do a serious injustice to the children in our community.

It is entirely possible that by the time you read these words, such a boycott has already taken place somewhere. Indeed, it is virtually certain that the following examples of activism in the late '90s and the first months of 2000 are incomplete. For an author, this fact is frustrating—and yet, in the current context, reassuring.

Even during what will eventually be viewed as the early stages of a backlash, parents, teachers, and students have been determined enough that the media have taken note. Hence such headlines as "Standardized Exams Coming Under Fire" (*USA Today*, June 11, 1999), "If These Are High Standards, We Don't Want Them" (*Christian Science Monitor*, Oct. 19, 1999), and "High-Stakes Testing: It's Backlash Time" (*U.S. News and World Report*, April 3, 2000), to name but three. Parents in Wisconsin successfully lobbied their state legislators to prevent a high school exit exam from being the sole determinant of whether students are permitted to graduate— a stinging defeat for Governor Tommy Thompson. In Florida, where schools are graded on the basis of test scores, with successful schools receiving more money and the neediest schools threatened with a loss of funding, a group of teachers and their principal at an "A" school (Gulf Gate Elementary) publicly refused to accept their bonuses. In a similar protest in North Carolina, teachers (at East Chapel Hill High School) pooled their state bonus checks and formed a foundation to send grants to the state's poorer schools.

There's more: Parents and teachers have taken to the streets in Colorado and Ohio. Lawsuits have been filed in Louisiana and Nevada to challenge the legality of high-stakes tests. (The first case to go to trial, in Texas, was decided in favor of the state.) Petitions are being circulated, locally and nationally; legislators are being lobbied; websites are being set up in several states to help testing opponents coordinate their efforts.[124] And individuals are challenging the system in a variety of ways. In early 1999, George Schmidt, a veteran Chicago high school teacher, published some of that city's tests (after students had already taken them) in a small independent newspaper so that the public could evaluate the validity and value of the questions. He was promptly charged with "gross disruption of the educational process," suspended without pay, and sued for $1.4 million.

Eugene Garcia, dean of the school of education at the University of California, Berkeley, resigned his position on an advisory committee to the State Board of Education. He did so to protest—and draw attention to—the Board's decision to subject students with limited English proficiency to tests on which they are certain to do poorly just because they don't speak the language. He then called for parents of such students to decline to participate in the testing program, thereby increasing the number of English-speaking students who would score below the median (since the state's high-stakes test, incredibly, is norm-referenced). These results, he speculated, might shock some of these families into opposing the tests.

Most impressive, and most dramatic, has been the growing number of boycotts all across the nation. Parents have said, in effect, "Not with my child you don't!" and refused to allow their children to take the tests. At first in scattered fashion—reflecting the lack of coordination among people who had independently decided the exams were destructive—students either declined to take them or failed them on purpose. This happened as long ago as 1989 in Torrance, California, and two years later in a parent-led protest involving several Colorado districts. Then, in 1998–99, parents across Michigan exempted 22.5 percent of students from the high school proficiency portion of the Michigan Educational Assessment Program (MEAP). Some districts had up to 90 percent of their students waived from taking the test, suggesting a "grassroots revolt by parents and students."[125] The following year, high school students walked out on a test in Marin County, California, calling it unjust that non-English-speaking students would have to take an English-language test, while students at the Whitney Young Magnet School in Chicago deliberately flunked the Illinois exam, saying they "refused to feed this test-taking frenzy." That same year, there were protests in Danvers, Cambridge, and Newton, Massachusetts, and in Merton, Wisconsin. As this book goes to press, a genuine boycott movement has spread across Massachusetts, with hundreds of students sitting out that state's required tests in the spring of 2000 as the result of a student-led campaign, while something similar is beginning to happen in Illinois.

Less because of boycotts than because decision makers are starting to realize how many students would be denied a diploma—or are, in fact, being held back a year—there has been some tinkering with the tests. It appears that more states will step back from the brink, particularly when it becomes clear that affluent, white students may be affected. Some test backers grudgingly concede that they may have moved a little too quickly, and now we are witnessing a delay of implementation here, a lower passing grade there, some sanctions waived and some expectations softened.[126] This tentative response has already begun to generate a counterreaction from hard-core pundits and politicians who affect a macho tone and taunt those responsible for "dumbing down" the tests and giving in to pressure groups (such as alarmed parents). As a harsh, punitive approach begins to reveal itself as counterproductive, this contingent has responded by demanding an even harsher, more punitive response.

In fact, though, the problem with this back pedaling is that it doesn't go nearly deep enough. Those who understand the weaknesses of standardized tests—and, indeed, the deficiencies of the whole tougher standards sensibility—will derive scant comfort from efforts to adjust the scores required for passing or to tinker with the applications of rewards and punishments. These minor repairs don't address the underlying problems with using such exams to judge students and educators, much less to bully them into higher scores. We are not quibbling about how high or how fast; we are calling the whole enterprise into question. We are not proposing to make school easier, but to make it better—and that requires rethinking standardized testing itself.

#37

NOTES

1. Resnick and Nolan, 1995, p. 102.

2. "Short-answer questions and computational exercises presented in formats that can be scored quickly and 'objectively'" represent a "typically American style of testing [that] is quite different from traditions in other countries, where more complex problem solving is the norm on both classroom and external examinations" (Schoen et al., 1999, p. 446).

3. See Rothstein, 1998; Bracey, 1997; and Berliner and Biddle, 1995, esp. chap. 2. As proof of the inadequacy of U.S. schools, many writers and public officials pointed to the sputtering condition of the U.S. economy. As far as I know, none of them subsequently apologized for offering a mistaken and unfair attack on our educational system once the economy recovered, nor did anyone credit teachers for the turnaround.

4. Frederiksen, 1984, p. 201.

5. McNeil, 1986, p. xviii.

6. Mitchell, 1992, p. 115.

7. My thinking on these questions (among others) has been greatly influenced by Deborah Meier.

8. Haney and Scott, 1987; Meier, 1981.

9. David Owen's 1985 critique, *None of the Above*, is still a good source of information about the SAT. After having been out of print for a number of years, it was recently revised and reissued with the help of Marilyn Doerr (Owen, 1999). Also see Sacks, 1999. And for a list of schools that don't require applicants to take the SAT or ACT, contact FairTest at (617) 864-4810.

10. You want proof? We've got proof. A study of math scores on the 1992 NAEP found that the combination of four variables that had nothing to do with instruction (number of parents living at home, parents' educational background, type of community [e.g., "disadvantaged urban," "extreme rural"], and state poverty rate) explained a whop-

ping 89 percent of the differences in state scores. In fact, one of those variables, the number of students who had one parent living at home, accounted for 71 percent of the variance all by itself (Robinson and Brandon, 1994). Within states, the same pattern holds. In Massachusetts, five factors explained 90 percent of the variance in scores on the state's MCAS exam, leading a researcher to conclude that students' performance "has almost everything to do with parental socioeconomic backgrounds and less to do with teachers, curricula, or what the children learned in the classroom" (Clancy, 2000). Another study looked just at the poverty level in each of 593 districts in Ohio and found a .80 correlation with 1997 scores on that state's proficiency test, meaning that this measure alone (which didn't even include other nonschool factors) explained nearly two thirds of the differences in test results (Hoover, 2000). In Edmonton, in the Canadian province of Alberta, socioeconomic status "was by far the strongest predictor, accounting for the vast majority" of variability in grade three and grade six achievement test scores in 1996 (Rogers, 1997). Even a quick look at the grades given to Florida schools under that state's new rating system found that "no school where less than 10 percent of the students qualify for free lunch scored below a C, and no school where more than 80 percent of the students qualify scored above a C" (Wilgoren, 2000, p. A18). Then there's the SAT, which, far from being a measure of merit (sometimes pointedly contrasted with affirmative action criteria), is largely a measure of family income. Break down the test takers by income, measured in $10,000 increments, and without exception the scores rise with each jump in parents' earnings ("1999 College Bound Seniors' Test Scores," 1999; the information is also available at www.collegeboard.org).

11. Ayers, 1993, p. 118.

12. Some commentators concede the relevance of poverty level and other socioeconomic factors, urging us to take into consideration how well schools or districts would be expected to perform based on their demographics so that we can then identify those that did better or worse than predicted. This allows us to congratulate poor schools with surprisingly high scores or condemn rich schools with surprisingly low scores. But such a strategy is based on the uncritical assumption that the tests themselves are valid and valuable measures of important learning. If, as I am about to argue, this is often not the case, then a high score may not be a particularly good sign, whether or not it's adjusted for socioeconomic status.

13. Resnick, 1987, p. 34.

14. See Frederiksen,1984, p. 199, for a discussion of Herbert Simon's distinction between well-structured and ill-structured problems, the

latter being more realistic and important, and the former showing up on standardized tests.

15. Resnick and Resnick, 1990, p. 71.

16. Madaus et al., 1992, p. 2.

17. Wood and Sellers, 1997, p. 181.

18. Bruce Alberts' comments, delivered at the Academy's annual meeting in May 1998, were reported in "Science Leader Criticizes Tests," 1998.

19. Cuoco and Ruopp, 1998.

20. Meece et al., 1988. The correlation was .28, significant at p 001.

21. The middle school students "who value literacy activities and who are task-focused toward literacy activities" got lower scores on the CTBS reading test (Anderman, 1992). And the same pattern showed up with high schoolers taking the SAT: researchers classified students' approaches to studying as "surface" (doing as little as possible and sticking to rote memorization), "deep" (understanding ideas and connecting new material to existing knowledge), or "achieving" (trying to get good grades and beat everyone else, without interest in what was being learned). It turned out that those who adopted a surface or achieving style did the best on the SAT. Scores were *negatively* correlated with a deep approach to learning (Hall et al., 1995).

22. Bracey, 1998a, p. 28.

23. One science teacher explained how it's necessary to "unteach some things" when test time rolls around: "If we teach creative thinking, if we teach analytical thinking, and if we teach children to look beyond the obvious into the not-quite-so-obvious, then the proficiency test comes and they think analytically, think beyond the obvious, and they will get [the questions] wrong because they know all of the exceptions to the rules and they say 'but what if. . . ?' And so I try to reserve at least a week prior to the proficiencies and throw everything aside and they check in their books and we close down the school and we give them proficiency drills." A history teacher does much the same thing, telling students they "just have to think, 'What's the least dumb answer here?' Do not try to use your mind on those" (McNeil, 2000, pp. 214-15).

24. Piaget, 1948/1973, p. 74.

25. Delisle, 1997, p. 44.

26. Peck et al., 1989.

27. Farr is quoted in Checkley, 1997, p. 5.

28. Frederiksen, 1984, p. 199. And from another source: "No multiple-choice question can be used to discover how well students can express their own ideas in their own words, how well they can marshal evidence to support their arguments, or how well they can adjust to the need to communicate for a particular purpose and to a particular audience. Nor can multiple-choice questions ever indicate whether what the student writes will be interesting to read" (Gertrude Conlan is quoted in Freedman, 1993, pp. 29–30).

29. Glovin, 1998; also see Fisher and Elliott, 2000. The company, Measurement, Inc., says that it has provided such "educational assessment services" for half the states, including New York, New Jersey, Ohio, Michigan, Colorado, Illinois, Connecticut, and every state in the south, stretching from Arizona to Florida and up to Maryland (see www.measinc.com/corpexp.htm).

30. "The use of standardized achievement tests with children, at least until the end of the third grade, is a definite no-no. The validity of score-based inferences that such testing will yield is likely to be inadequate" (Popham, 2000, p. 145). Careful observations of young children in a test-taking situation support this recommendation, offering evidence of just how much stress they feel and just how inappropriate such testing is at this age. One study quantified the extent of that stress for kindergartners and noted in passing that, apart from the emotional toll the process takes on the children, the pressure they feel also reduces the tests' validity. "During interviews conducted after the testing, the children were able to answer orally some of the questions they had marked incorrectly" (Fleege et al., 1992; quotation appears on p. 23. Also see Andersen, 1998 for a poignant account of second graders taking a test.).

31. NAEYC, 1987.

32. Jervis, 1989, p. 15.

33. Glaser, 1963, p. 520.

34. Popham, 1999, p. 10.

35. The reverse situation actually occurred in late 1998 on an international scale. A front-page *New York Times* article (Bronner, 1998, p. A1) began as follows: "A major new international study shows that American high school graduation rates, for generations the highest in the world, have slipped below those of most industrialized countries." The reporter then struggled to explain what has happened to our schools, quoting an academic who believes "we should be quite alarmed by this." (The same week, a front-page article in *Education*

Week [Hoff, 1998] carried the ominous headline "U.S. Graduation Rates Starting to Fall Behind.") It turned out, however, that the study in question actually reported no slippage in absolute terms; on most measures, the U.S. is actually doing better than ever. In 1990, an American five-year-old was expected to attend school for 16.3 years; six years later, that had increased to 16.8 years. Furthermore, 77 percent of Americans between the ages of fifty-five and sixty-four had completed "at least an upper-secondary education" in 1996, while 87 percent of a younger cohort (those between the ages of twenty-five and thirty-four) had done so. The drop in rank just reflected the improvement of other countries, which would be regarded as bad news only by someone who was more rivalrous than rational.

36. The technical term for what norm-referenced tests are designed to produce is "response variance." For a good discussion of these issues, see Popham, 1993, pp. 106–111 or Popham 2000, pp. 58–66.

37. For more on the effects of competition, see Kohn, 1992.

38. A survey of parents' understanding of a test in Michigan revealed that "an overwhelming majority . . . interpreted the criterion-referenced score as a normative percentile" (Paris et al., 1991, p. 14).

39. Popham, 1998, p. 383.

40. Ayers, 1993, p. 116.

41. Mitchell, 1992, p. 15; and Resnick and Resnick, 1990, p. 73, respectively.

42. Wolf et al., 1991, p. 46. Interestingly, an early version of the NAEP included a task that was presented to small groups of students in order to assess how proficient they were at working together. But this was dropped in subsequent years "in the face of rising costs as the NAEP become more concerned with expanding samples to make comparisons" (Coffman, 1993, p. 6).

43. Wiggins, 1993, p. 72. "Thoughtful and deep understanding is simply not assessable in secure testing," he continues, "and we will continue to send the message to teachers that simplistic recall or application, based on 'coverage,' is all that matters—until we change the policy of secrecy" (p. 92).

44. See, for example, Keller, 2000.

45. David Rogosa's calculations are reported in Viadero, 1999. For the original report, see www.cse.ucla.edu/CRESST/Reports/drrguide.html.

46. For more on this topic, see Kohn, 1993.

47. For reviews of the research, see Deci et al., 1999; Kohn, 1993; Deci and Ryan, 1985; Lepper and Greene, 1978.

48. McNeil, 2000, p. 225.

49. The extent of improvement in Texas, with respect to raising academic performance and reducing inequity, has been challenged by a number of investigations. Higher TAAS scores offer no evidence of progress, both because of the low quality of that test and because it has effectively hijacked the curriculum. The results on more meaningful indicators, such as the NAEP, have been mixed, depending on which subjects, which grade levels, and which time periods are analyzed. (An independent evaluation by the RAND Corporation casts further doubt about claims of higher levels of student proficiency.) What does seem clear is that the teaching of many topics—and, indeed, of entire subject areas, such as science—has been sacrificed in the quest to raise TAAS scores. The consequences appear to be most severe for poor and minority students, and disparities between dropout rates for African Americans and Latinos, on the one hand, and whites, on the other, suggest that the state is, in important respects, moving backward. For more, see McNeil and Valenzuela, 2000; McNeil, 2000; Schrag, 2000; Weisman, 2000; and Sacks, 1999, pp. 108–14.

50. Colvin, 1999.

51. Guthrie, 1999. For another example (Tacoma, Washington), see Sacks, 1999, pp. 140–51.

52. See, for example, Hoff, 2000a.

53. "Educators from the progressive tradition are often accused of 'experimenting' on kids. But never in the history of the nation have progressives proposed an experiment so drastic, vast, and potentially serious in its real-life impact on millions of young people [as what is being done in the name of standards and accountability]. If the consequences are other than those its supporters hope for, the harm to the nation's educational system and the youngsters involved— maybe even to our economy—will be large and hard to undo" (Meier, 2000, p. 12).

54. Quotation: Darling-Hammond, 1997, p. 238. Comparison of states: Neill and Gayler, 1999; also see Bracey, 1998b and Sacks, 1999, pp. 88–91. (There are no data yet on the effects of high-stakes testing for younger students, in which promotion to the next grade is contingent on a test score. The data referred to here are based on the admittedly unproven assumption that the states using graduation tests also place more emphasis on testing younger students, or at least that the impact of a graduation test is likely to trickle down. If you compare the change of each state's NAEP scores between 1992 and 1996, the existence of a high school exit exam made it no more

72

likely that fourth-grade results improved and made it *less* likely that eighth-grade results improved. Moreover, if you track a given cohort of students, comparing fourth graders in 1992 with eighth graders in 1996 [see Barton and Coley, 1998], the states whose students improved the most typically did not have high-stakes graduation exams at the time, while many of the states with the least growth did.) Other countries: Kellaghan et al., 1996; Freedman, 1995.

55. Flink et al., 1990.

56. Deci et al., 1982.

57. Steve Frommeyer is quoted in Keller, 1998, p. 16.

58. Berliner and Biddle, 1995, pp. 192–94.

59. See, for example, McGill-Franzen and Allington, 1993.

60. Jim May is quoted in Wilgoren, 2000, p. A18.

61. Watson, 1998.

62. Dorn, 1998, p. 16. Also see McNeil, 2000, pp. xxv-xxix, on how "the language of accountability usurps developmental, cultural, and democratic discourse."

63. Ryan and La Guardia, 1999, p. 46.

64. Calkins et al., 1998, pp. 2, 73.

65. This point is made by Stodolsky, cited in Noble and Smith, 1994.

66. Zemelman et al., 1998, p. 218.

67. In Texas districts "where schools' TAAS scores are tied to incentive pay for teachers or principals, and where TAAS-based contracts have replaced tenure, there is an even greater tendency for school personnel to shift dollars away from instruction and into the expensive TAAS-prep and 'alignment' materials and consultants. Again, frequently these incentives are applied in schools or districts whose populations are poor or minority or both." One desperately underfunded, largely Hispanic school, for example, spent "almost its entire instructional budget for a set of commercial test-prep materials and required even its best teachers to set aside their high-quality lessons and replace them with the test-prep materials. Scores on some sections of the TAAS did go up, but teachers report that students' actual capacity to read, to handle high school level assignments, to engage in serious thought and be able to follow through on work actually declined" (McNeil and Valenzuela, 2000, pp. 8, 10).

68. Darling-Hammond's analogy is cited in Calkins et al., 1998, p. 44.

69. Hoff, 2000b.

70. Sacks, 1999, p. 138.

71. McNeil, 2000, pp. 203, 204.

72. Feld, 2000, p. 1A.

73. Jones and Whitford, 1997, p. 280. Also see Frederiksen on this point.

74. Wellstone, 2000. Here's how journalist Peter Sacks (p. 158) put it: "If social engineers had set out to invent a virtually perfect inequality machine, designed to perpetuate class and race divisions . . . those engineers could do no better than the present-day accountability systems already put to use in American schools."

75. It is theoretically possible that tests could be written to favor the sort of out-of-school knowledge acquired in the inner city, thereby offering an advantage to students who grow up there. Somehow, though, this rarely turns out to be the case.

76. Neill and Medina, 1989, p. 692.

77. "Racial Bias Built into Tests," 1999–2000, p. 10.

78. See note 67.

79. For proof, see Madaus et al., 1992; Herman and Golan, 1993.

80. Strickland is quoted in Routman, 1996, p. 43.

81. See also McNeil, 2000: "If year after year, minority children are subjected to test-prep activities and materials in lieu of the regular curriculum experienced by middle-class and suburban students, then the system will be exacerbating the academic weaknesses in these children. . . . The longer standardized controls are in place, the wider the gap becomes" (pp. 3, 248).

82. Wellstone, 2000.

83. Put aside for a moment the limits of standardized tests. Put aside the question of how many students really are graduated without knowing how to write a coherent paragraph or make change for a dollar. Put aside the matter of where the fault lies when that does happen. Simply consider the worst-case bottom-line choice, in the absence of remediation and school improvement: a clueless eighteen-year-old who receives a high school diploma versus a clueless eighteen-year-old from whom a high school diploma is withheld. Who is in worse shape? To oversimplify, the former may be in for a rude shock when he or she starts work, but the latter may never get the chance to start work. So is it concern about the well-being of these

youngsters or something else entirely that motivates relatively privileged people to demand that we get tough and set the bar higher?

84. Interviews with fifty teachers identified as being exceptional at their
craft revealed a consistent lack of emphasis on testing, if not a deliberate decision to minimize the practice. See Jackson, 1968/1990.

85. See, for example, Sizer, 1992.

86. On this topic, see Le Countryman and Schroeder, 1996; and Stiggins, 1994, pp. 418–21. (The latter book is a useful reference on
the whole question of alternative classroom assessment.) There's no
reason students can't also be involved in *written* evaluations of their
own learning rather than leaving that up to the teacher (see Routman, 1996, pp. 159–63).

87. For a useful discussion of these and other issues pertaining to alternative assessments, see Neill et al., 1995.

88. Information about the Learning Record (originally adapted from the
Primary Language Record, developed in England) is available from
the Center for Language in Learning, 10610 Quail Canyon Road,
El Cajon, CA, 92021, or at www.learningrecord.org. Also see Barr
et al., 1999; Barr, 2000. Information about Work Sampling is available from Rebus, Inc., PO Box 4479, Ann Arbor, MI, 48106, or
by calling 1-800-435-3085, or at www.rebusinc.com. Also see
Meisels, 1993.

89. Rose and Gallup, 1999, p. 52.

90. In a *Los Angeles Times* poll, more than half the parents surveyed (54
percent) said they believed that teacher evaluations "are better indicators of a child's progress in school" than are standardized tests, while
fewer than one in five thought the reverse was true. Most of the remain-
der thought the two were of equal value (Sahagun, 2000, p. A22).
Skepticism about standardized tests is rampant even in the absence of
comparisons with other forms of assessment. A Harris Interactive
national on-line survey conducted in April 2000 found that more than
half of parents who lived in the states with high-stakes exams (and fully
three-fifths of those who lived elsewhere) believed that such tests are
not "a true and valid measurement" of their child's ability. Only 22 and
25 percent of parents in those respective types of states thought the
tests were a good measure. (Available at www.ascd.org/educationnews/
pr/sylvan.html.) The following month, in a Luntz/Laszlo poll of eight
hundred registered voters, fewer than one out of three agreed with the
statement "A student's progress for one school year can be accurately
summarized by a single standardized test." (Forty-two percent strongly
disagreed and another 20 percent somewhat disagreed.) A plurality of

those surveyed even disagreed that such "test scores accurately reflect what children know about the subject being tested." (Available at www.aasa.org/issues/stand-test/sld001.htm.)

91. Shepard and Bliem, 1995.

92. Neill and Medina, 1989, p. 695.

93. Originally published in the September 1996 issue of *Educational Leadership*, "What to Look for in a Classroom" appears as a chart in Kohn, 1999, Appendix B.

94. Howe, 1994, p. 31.

95. Central Park East, 1993, p. 24.

96. A thoughtful proposal for what alternative assessment might look like as a matter of state policy was published as *A Call for an Authentic Statewide Assessment System*, drafted by the Massachusetts Coalition for Authentic Reform in Education (CARE), and is available at www.fairtest.org/care/accountability.html or www.alfiekohn.org/teaching/aa.htm, or by writing FairTest, 342 Broadway, Cambridge, MA 02139.

97. Haertel, 1999, p. 663.

98. Jones, 1998. Two other authors point out that "measurement-driven instruction" is "merely an extension of behaviorist psychology," so when policy makers continue to depend on "coercion to create uniformity"—except now as a way to get higher-quality instruction—they create a fatal inconsistency between what is done to teachers and what teachers are expected to do with students (Noble and Smith, 1994).

99. On this point, see Airasian, 1988.

100. For more on this distinction, see Kohn, 1999, chap. 2 and the work of Carol Dweck, Carole Ames, John Nicholls, and other educational psychologists.

101. Maehr and Midgley, 1996, p. 7. This is a point frequently overlooked by educators who promote more "authentic" assessments without attending to the psychological impact of evaluation itself.

102. Rothman, 1995, p. 153. For other, related problems with using performance assessments for accountability purposes, see Haertel's article in its entirety and Madaus and O'Dwyer, 1999.

103. Monty Neill, personal communication, 2000.

104. Daniels, 1993, p. 5.

105. Karnes et al., 1983.

106. Smith, 1994, p. 29.

107. See Taylor and Walton, 1998; and Calkins et al., 1998. Several articles in the December 1996/January 1997 issue of *Educational Leadership* are also relevant.

108. McNeil, 2000, p. xxvi.

109. Kozol, 2000, p. x.

110. These and other problems with the "tougher standards" movement are explored at greater length in Kohn, 1999. Also see Ohanian, 1999 and Meier, 2000.

111. Olson, 2000, p. 12. Emphasis added.

112. "No single test score can be considered a definitive measure of a student's knowledge," so "an educational decision that will have a major impact on a test taker should not be made solely or automatically on the basis of a single test score. Other relevant information about the student's knowledge and skills should also be taken into account" (Heubert and Hauser, 1999).

113. For example, one Republican state legislator in Delaware announced: "I cannot support, under any circumstances, a test that will be the be-all and end-all of a student's [getting a diploma]. So why don't we just remove that? How have we ever got to the point where we allow one test to determine our children's future?" At that point in the debate, according to a newspaper account, "several in the chamber spoke of how they had successfully moved from high school through college to even advanced degrees without having to pass a single, difficult, standardized test. Others recalled conversations with teachers who admitted they would not be successful taking the tests themselves. 'It seems like we're trying to treat the symptom instead of the disease,'" another Republican representative remarked, adding, " 'The problem is the testing' " (Eldred, 2000). Similarly, Pennsylvania's state board of education ruled out a test to determine whether students would receive a diploma, with one board member commenting, "I couldn't sit here in this seat and take that kind of decision out of the hands of teachers who had worked hard with the students for 13 years" (Newton, 2000).

114. This argument in particular resonates with people across the political spectrum.

115. For further thoughts on helping educators to become more adept at political organizing, see Brinkley and Weaver, 1998.

116. Popham, 2000, p. 284.

117. One bumper sticker now being circulated is rather tentative, asking: IS STANDARDIZED TESTING HURTING OUR KIDS? Another, more decisive one features the initials of the state's test in a circle with a red diagonal slash running through them, followed by: THESE TESTS HURT KIDS! Some educators, meanwhile, have printed up T-shirts reading: HIGH STAKES ARE FOR TOMATOES.

118. Paris et al., 1991, p. 17.

119. Davis, 1999.

120. Hegarty, 2000.

121. Lewis, 1995, pp. 201, 16.

122. Coles, 1994. Quotations are taken from pp. 16, 23.

123. This account is based on Lord, 1999; Hayward, 2000; and personal communications. Bougas received a two-week suspension without pay in May 2000 but, at this writing, still has his job. At least two other Massachusetts teachers—Susan Frommer and Tom Hooper, both at Lincoln-Sudbury High School—have also refused to administer the MCAS, so far without repercussions.

124. For example, AZ: www.azstandards.org; CA: www.calcare.org; FL: www.angelfire.com/fl4/fcar; GA (Gwinnett County): www.cpoga .org; MA: www.caremass.org; MD: www.geocities.com/stophsa; MI: www.pipeline.com/~rgibson/meap.html; NC: www.geocities.com/ nccds/index.html; OH: www.stopopts.org; TX: www.texastesting .org; VA: www.SOLreform.com; and WA: www.rereformed.com. Also check out these national sites (in addition to www.alfiekohn.org and www.fairtest.org): www.pencilsdown.org and www.nomore tests.com (student-oriented).

125. Van Moorlehem, 1998. Overall, "those opting out of the test tend to be average or above-average students," some of whom wore T-shirts that urged their peers to "just say no" to the test (Ibid.).

126. See, for example, Steinberg, 1999.

FURTHER READING

Recent Books

Linda M. McNeil, *Contradictions of School Reform: Educational Costs of Standardized Testing*. New York: Routledge, 2000.

Deborah Meier, *Will Standards Save Public Education?* Boston: Beacon, 2000.

Susan Ohanian, *One Size Fits Few: The Folly of Educational Standards*. Portsmouth, N.H.: Heinemann, 1999.

W. James Popham, *Testing! Testing!: What Every Parent Should Know About School Tests*. Boston: Allyn and Bacon, 2000.

Betty Lou Whitford and Ken Jones, *Accountability, Assessment, and Teacher Commitment: Lessons from Kentucky's Reform Efforts*. Albany: State University of New York Press, 2000.

Peter Sacks, *Standardized Minds: The High Price of America's Testing Culture and What We Can Do to Change It*. Cambridge, Mass.: Perseus, 1999.

Gerald Bracey, *Put to the Test: An Educator's and Consumer's Guide to Standardized Testing*. Bloomington, Ind.: Phi Delta Kappa, 1998.

Favorite Articles

W. James Popham, "Why Standardized Tests Don't Measure Educational Quality." *Educational Leadership*, March 1999: 8–15.

Scott G. Paris, Theresa A. Lawton, Julianne C. Turner, and Jodie L. Roth, "A Developmental Perspective on Standardized Achievement Testing." *Educational Researcher*, June–July 1991: 12–20, 40.

Mary Lee Smith, "Put to the Test: The Effects of External Testing on Teachers." *Educational Researcher*, June–July 1991: 8–11.

D. Monty Neill and Noe J. Medina, "Standardized Testing: Harmful to Educational Health." *Phi Delta Kappan*, May 1989: 688–97.

Lorrie A. Shepard, "Why We Need Better Assessments." *Educational Leadership.* April 1989: 4–9.

Norman Frederiksen, "The Real Test Bias: Influences of Testing on Teaching and Learning." *American Psychologist,* March 1984: 193–202.

Deborah Meier, "Why Reading Tests Don't Test Reading." *Dissent,* Fall 1981: 457–66.

On the Ambiguity of Test Questions

Walt Haney and Laurie Scott, "Talking with Children About Tests: An Exploratory Study of Test Item Ambiguity." In *Cognitive and Linguistic Analyses of Test Performance,* edited by Roy O. Freedle and Richard P. Duran. Norwood, NJ: Ablex, 1987.

David Owen with Marilyn Doerr, *None of the Above: The Truth Behind the SATs.* Lanham, Md.: Rowman and Littlefield, 1999.

Deborah Meier, "Why Reading Tests Don't Test Reading." *Dissent,* Fall 1981: 457–66.

Banesh Hoffmann, *The Tyranny of Testing.* New York, NY: Crowell-Collier, 1962.

On How to Make the Best of a Bad Thing

Kathe Taylor and Sherry Walton, *Children at the Center: A Workshop Approach to Standardized Test Preparation, K–8.* Portsmouth, N.H.: Heinemann, 1998.

Lucy Calkins, Kate Montgomery, and Donna Santman, *A Teacher's Guide to Standardized Reading Tests: Knowledge Is Power.* Portsmouth, N.H.: Heinemann, 1998.

On Watching Children Taking Tests

Susan R. Andersen, "The Trouble with Testing." *Young Children,* July 1998: 25–29.

James R. Delisle, "Proficient at What?" *Education Week,* 20 May 1998: 37, 39.

Indispensable Periodical

FairTest Examiner—quarterly newsletter available from FairTest, 342 Broadway, Cambridge, MA 02139. Also contact this organization (www.fairtest.org) to join the Assessment Reform Network listserv.

Important Website That Just Happens to Be Named After the Author

www.alfiekohn.org, then click on "Standards and Testing"

REFERENCES

Airasian, Peter W. "Measurement Driven Instruction: A Closer Look." *Educational Measurement: Issues and Practice* 7, 4 (1988): 6–11.

Anderman, Eric M. "Motivation and Cognitive Strategy Use in Reading and Writing." Paper presented at the National Reading Conference, San Antonio, Tex., December 1992.

Andersen, Susan R. "The Trouble with Testing." *Young Children*, July 1998: 25–29.

Ayers, William. *To Teach: The Journey of a Teacher.* New York: Teachers College Press, 1993.

Barr, Mary A. "Looking at the Learning Record." *Educational Leadership*, February 2000: 20–24.

Barr, Mary A., Dana A. Craig, Dolores Fisette, and Margaret A. Syverson. *Assessing Literacy with the Learning Record.* Portsmouth, N.H.: Heinemann, 1999.

Barton, Paul E., and Richard J. Coley. *Growth in School: Achievement Gains from the Fourth to the Eighth Grade.* Princeton, N.J.: Educational Testing Service, 1998.

Berliner, David C., and Bruce J. Biddle. *The Manufactured Crisis: Myths, Fraud, and the Attack on America's Public Schools.* Reading, Mass.: Addison-Wesley, 1995.

Bracey, Gerald W. *Setting the Record Straight : Responses to Misconceptions About Public Education in the United States.* Alexandria, Va.: Association for Supervision and Curriculum Development, 1997.

———. *Put to the Test: An Educator's and Consumer's Guide to Standardized Testing.* Bloomington, Ind.: Phi Delta Kappa, 1998a.

———. "High Stakes Testing Comes a Cropper?" *Phi Delta Kappan*, April 1998b: 630.

Brinkley, Ellen H., and Constance Weaver. "Organizing for Political Action: Suggestions from Experience." In *In Defense of Good Teach-*

ing: What Teachers Need to Know About the "Reading Wars," edited by Kenneth S. Goodman. Portsmouth, N.H.: Heinemann, 1998.

Bronner, Ethan. "Long a Leader, U.S. Now Lags in High School Graduate Rate." *New York Times*, 24 November 1998: A1, A18.

Calkins, Lucy, Kate Montgomery, and Donna Santman. *A Teacher's Guide to Standardized Reading Tests: Knowledge Is Power.* Portsmouth, N.H.: Heinemann, 1998.

Central Park East Secondary School. "CPESS Graduation Handbook." Unpublished document. New York, 1993.

Checkley, Kathy. "Assessment That Serves Instruction." *ASCD Education Update*, June 1997: 1, 4–6.

Clancy, Kevin J. "Making More Sense of MCAS Scores." *Boston Globe*, 24 April 2000: A19.

Coffman, William E. "A King over Egypt, Which Knew Not Joseph." *Educational Measurement: Issues and Practice* 12, 2 (1993): 5–8, 23.

Coles, Jane. "Enough Was Enough: The Teachers' Boycott of National Curriculum Testing." *Changing English* (published by the University of London's Institute of Education), 1, 2 (1994): 16–31.

Colvin, Richard Lee. "Texas Schools Gain Notice and Skepticism." *Los Angeles Times*, 6 July 1999.

Cuoco, Al, and Faye Ruopp. "Math Exam Rationale Doesn't Add Up." *Boston Globe*, 24 May 1998: D3.

Daniels, Harvey. "Whole Language: What's the Fuss?" *Rethinking Schools*, Winter 1993: 4–7.

Darling-Hammond, Linda. *The Right to Learn: A Blueprint for Creating Schools That Work.* San Francisco: Jossey-Bass, 1997.

Davis, Anne. "Executives in West Bend Struggle with Sample of State Graduation Test." *Milwaukee Journal Sentinel*, 20 January 1999.

Deci, Edward L., Richard Koestner, and Richard M. Ryan. "A Meta-Analytic Review of Experiments Examining the Effects of Extrinsic Rewards on Intrinsic Motivation." *Psychological Bulletin* 125 (1999): 627–68.

Deci, Edward L., and Richard M. Ryan. *Intrinsic Motivation and Self-Determination in Human Behavior.* New York: Plenum, 1985.

Deci, Edward L., Nancy H. Spiegel, Richard M. Ryan, Richard Koestner, and Manette Kauffman. "Effects of Performance Standards on Teaching Styles: Behavior of Controlling Teachers." *Journal of Educational Psychology* 74 (1982): 852–59.

Delisle, James R. "How Proficiency Tests Fall Short: (Let Me Count the Ways)." *Education Week*, 2 April 1997: 41, 44.

Dorn, Sherman. "The Political Legacy of School Accountability Systems." *Education Policy Analysis Archives* 6, 1 (1998): 1–34. (Available at http://olam.ed.asu.edu/epaa/v6n1.html.)

Eldred, Tom. "Education Bill Passes Delaware House." *Delaware State News*, 17 March 2000.

Feld, Jayne J. "Mentorship Programs May Become Casualties." *Journal News*, 24 April 2000: 1A, 5A.

Fisher, Mark, and Scott Elliott. "Proficiency: The Test Questioned." *Dayton Daily News*, 13 March 2000.

Fleege, Pamela O., Rosalind Charlesworth, Diane C. Burts, and Craig H. Hart. "Stress Begins in Kindergarten: A Look at Behavior During Standardized Testing." *Journal of Research in Child Education* 7 (1992): 20–26.

Flink, Cheryl, Ann K. Boggiano, and Marty Barrett. "Controlling Teacher Strategies: Undermining Children's Self-Determination and Performance." *Journal of Personality and Social Psychology* 59 (1990): 916–24.

Frederiksen, Norman. "The Real Test Bias: Influences of Testing on Teaching and Learning." *American Psychologist* 39, 3 (1984): 193–202.

Freedman, Sarah Warshauer. "Linking Large-Scale Testing and Classroom Portfolio Assessments of Student Writing." *Educational Assessment* 1 (1993): 27–52.

———. "Exam-Based Reform Stifles Student Writing in the U.K." *Educational Leadership*, March 1995: 26–29.

Glaser, Robert. "Instructional Technology and the Measurement of Learning Outcomes: Some Questions." *American Psychologist* 18 (1963): 519–21.

Glovin, David. "Low-Paid Part-Timers Judge N.J. Students." *The Record* [of Hackensack, N.J.], 29 November 1998.

Guthrie, Julian. "Improvement May Be Smoke and Mirrors." *San Francisco Examiner*, 12 April 1999.

Haertel, Edward H. "Performance Assessment and Education Reform." *Phi Delta Kappan*, May 1999: 662–66.

Hall, Cathy W., Larry M. Bolen, and Robert H. Gupton, Jr. "Predictive Validity of the Study Process Questionnaire for Undergraduate Students." *College Student Journal* 29 (1995): 234–39.

Haney, Walt, and Laurie Scott. "Talking with Children About Tests: An Exploratory Study of Test Item Ambiguity." In *Cognitive and Linguistic Analyses of Test Performance*, edited by Roy O. Freedle and Richard P. Duran. Norwood, N.J.: Ablex, 1987.

Hayward, Ed. "MCAS Opponents Hold Rally in Hub." *Boston Herald*, 16 May 2000.

Hegarty, Stephen. "Officials Dodge FCAT Dare." *St. Petersburg Times*, 13 February 2000.

Herman, Joan L., and Shari Golan. "The Effects of Standardized Testing on Teaching and Schools." *Educational Measurement: Issues and Practice* 12, 4 (1993): 20–25, 41–42.

Heubert, Jay P., and Robert M. Hauser, eds. *High Stakes: Testing for Tracking, Promotion, and Graduation*. Washington, D.C.: National Academy Press, 1999.

Hoff, David J. "U. S. Graduation Rates Starting to Fall Behind." *Education Week*, 25 November 1998: 1, 11.

———. "Testing's Ups and Downs Predictable: Research Shows Cyclical Pattern." *Education Week*, 26 January 2000a: 1, 12.

———. "Test Scores May Be Misleading, Experts Warn." *Education Week*, 5 April 2000b: 10.

Hoover, Randy L. "Forces and Factors Affecting Ohio Proficiency Test Performance." 2000. Published on-line at http://cc.ysu.edu/~rlhoover/OPT.

Howe, Kenneth R. "Standards, Assessment, and Equality of Educational Opportunity." *Educational Researcher*, November 1994: 27–33.

Jackson, Philip W. *Life in Classrooms*. 1968. Reprint. New York: Teachers College Press, 1990.

Jervis, Kathe. "Daryl Takes a Test." *Educational Leadership*, April 1989: 10–15.

Jones, Ken. "Teacher Accountability: High Resolution, Not High Stakes." *Mathematics Education Dialogues* (published by the National Council of Teachers of Mathematics), May/June 1998: 10.

Jones, Ken, and Betty Lou Whitford. "Kentucky's Conflicting Reform Principles: High-Stakes School Accountability and Student Performance Assessment." *Phi Delta Kappan*, December 1997: 276–81.

Karnes, Merle B., Allan M. Shwedel, and Mark B. Williams. "A Comparison of Five Approaches for Educating Young Children from Low-Income Homes." In *As the Twig Is Bent . . . : Lasting Effects of*

Preschool Programs, edited by The Consortium for Longitudinal Studies. Hillsdale, N.J.: Erlbaum, 1983.

Kellaghan, Thomas, George F. Madaus, and Anastasia Raczek. *The Use of External Examinations to Improve Student Motivation*. Washington, D.C.: American Educational Research Association, 1996.

Keller, Bess. "In Age of Accountability, Principals Feel the Heat." *Education Week*, 20 May 1998: 1, 16.

———. "Incentives for Test-Takers Run the Gamut." *Education Week*, 3 May 2000: 1, 28.

Kohn, Alfie. *No Contest: The Case Against Competition*. Rev. ed. Boston: Houghton Mifflin, 1992.

———. *Punished by Rewards: The Trouble with Gold Stars, Incentive Plans, A's, Praise, and Other Bribes*. Boston: Houghton Mifflin, 1993.

———. *The Schools Our Children Deserve: Moving Beyond Traditional Classrooms and "Tougher Standards."* Boston: Houghton Mifflin, 1999.

Kozol, Jonathan. Foreword to *Will Standards Save Public Education?* by Deborah Meier. Boston: Beacon, 2000.

Le Countryman, Lyn, and Merrie Schroeder. "When Students Lead Parent-Teacher Conferences." *Educational Leadership*, April 1996: 64–68.

Lepper, Mark R., and David Greene, eds. *The Hidden Costs of Rewards: New Perspectives on the Psychology of Human Motivation*. Hillsdale, N.J.: Erlbaum, 1978.

Lewis, Catherine C. *Educating Hearts and Minds: Reflections on Japanese Preschool and Elementary Education*. Cambridge, England: Cambridge University Press, 1995.

Lord, Robin. "Harwich Teacher Refused to Hand Out MCAS Test." *Cape Cod Times*, 3 June 1999.

Madaus, George F., and Laura M. O'Dwyer. "A Short History of Performance Assessment." *Phi Delta Kappan*, May 1999: 688–95.

Madaus, George F., Mary Maxwell West, Maryellen C. Harmon, Richard G. Lomax, and Katherine A. Viator. *The Influence of Testing on Teaching Math and Science in Grades 4–12: Executive Summary*. Boston: Center for the Study of Testing, Evaluation, and Educational Policy, 1992.

Maehr, Martin L., and Carol Midgley. *Transforming School Cultures*. Boulder, Col.: Westview, 1996.

McGill-Franzen, Anne, and Richard L. Allington. "Flunk 'em or Get Them Classified: The Contamination of Primary Grade Accountability Data." *Educational Researcher*, January–February 1993: 19–22.

McNeil, Linda M. *Contradictions of Control: School Structure and School Knowledge*. New York: Routledge & Kegan Paul, 1986.

————. *Contradictions of School Reform: Educational Costs of Standardized Testing*. New York: Routledge, 2000.

McNeil, Linda M., and Angela Valenzuela. *The Harmful Impact of the TAAS System of Testing in Texas: Beneath the Accountability Rhetoric*. Cambridge, Mass.: Harvard University Civil Rights Project, 2000. (Available at: www.law.harvard.edu/groups/civilrights/testing.html.)

Meece, Judith L., Phyllis C. Blumenfeld, and Rick H. Hoyle. "Students' Goal Orientations and Cognitive Engagement in Classroom Activities." *Journal of Educational Psychology* 80 (1988): 514–23.

Meier, Deborah. "Why Reading Tests Don't Test Reading." *Dissent*, Fall 1981: 457–66.

————. *Will Standards Save Public Education?* Boston: Beacon, 2000.

Meisels, Samuel J. "Remaking Classroom Assessment with the Work Sampling System." *Young Children*, July 1993: 34–40.

Mitchell, Ruth. *Testing for Learning: How New Approaches to Evaluation Can Improve American Schools*. New York: Free Press, 1992.

National Association for the Education of Young Children. "Standardized Testing of Young Children 3 through 8 Years of Age." Position Statement. Washington, D.C.: NAEYC, 1987.

Neill, [D.] Monty, Phyllis Bursh, Bob Schaeffer, Carolyn Thall, Marilyn Yohe, and Pamela Zappardino. *Implementing Performance Assessments: A Guide to Classroom, School and System Reform*. Cambridge, Mass.: FairTest, 1995.

Neill, D. Monty, and Keith Gayler. *Do High Stakes Graduation Tests Improve Learning Outcomes?* Cambridge, Mass.: Harvard University Civil Rights Project, 1999. (Available at www.law.harvard.edu/groups/civilrights/conferences/testing98/drafts.html.)

Neill, D. Monty, and Noe J. Medina. "Standardized Testing: Harmful to Educational Health." *Phi Delta Kappan*, May 1989: 688–97.

Newton, Christopher. "State Education Board Rules Out High School Test." *Philadelphia Inquirer*, 20 April 2000.

"1999 College Bound Seniors' Test Scores: SAT." *FairTest Examiner*, Fall 1999: 13.

Noble, Audrey J., and Mary Lee Smith. "Old and New Beliefs About Measurement-Driven Reform: 'The More Things Change, the More They Stay the Same'." CSE Technical Report 373. Los Angeles: National Center for Research on Evaluation, Standards, and Student Testing (CRESST), 1994. (Available at http://cresst96.cse.ucla.edu/Reports/TECH373.PDF.)

Ohanian, Susan. *One Size Fits Few: The Folly of Educational Standards.* Portsmouth, N.H.: Heinemann, 1999.

Olson, Lynn. "Worries of a Standards 'Backlash' Grow." *Education Week,* 5 April 2000: 1, 12–13.

Owen, David, with Marilyn Doerr. *None of the Above: The Truth Behind the SATs.* Rev. ed. Lanham, Md.: Rowman and Littlefield, 1999.

Paris, Scott G., Theresa A. Lawton, Julianne C. Turner, and Jodie L. Roth. "A Developmental Perspective on Standardized Achievement Testing." *Educational Researcher,* June–July 1991: 12–20.

Peck, Donald M., Stanley M. Jencks, and Michael L. Connell. "Improving Instruction Through Brief Interviews." *Arithmetic Teacher,* November 1989: 15–17.

Piaget, Jean. *To Understand Is to Invent: The Future of Education.* Originally published 1948. New York: Grossman, 1973.

Popham, W. James. *Educational Evaluation.* 3d ed. Boston: Allyn & Bacon, 1993.

———. "Farewell, Curriculum." *Phi Delta Kappan,* January 1998: 380–84.

———. "Why Standardized Tests Don't Measure Educational Quality." *Educational Leadership,* March 1999: 8–15.

———. *Testing! Testing!: What Every Parent Should Know About School Tests.* Boston: Allyn and Bacon, 2000.

"Racial Bias Built into Tests." *FairTest Examiner,* Winter 1999–2000: 10–11.

Resnick, Lauren B. *Education and Learning to Think.* Washington, D.C.: National Academy Press, 1987.

Resnick, Lauren B., and Katherine J. Nolan. "Standards for Education." In *Debating the Future of American Education: Do We Need National Standards and Assessments?* edited by Diane Ravitch. Washington, D.C.: Brookings Institution, 1995.

Resnick, Lauren B., and Daniel P. Resnick. "Tests as Standards of Achievement in Schools." In *The Uses of Standardized Tests in Amer-*

ican Education: Proceedings of the 1989 ETS Invitational Conference. Princeton, N.J.: Educational Testing Service, 1990.

Robinson, Glen E., and David P. Brandon. *NAEP Test Scores: Should They Be Used to Compare and Rank State Educational Quality?* Arlington, Va.: Educational Research Service, 1994.

Rogers, Todd. Unpublished data, University of Alberta.(Summarized in *Alberta Teachers Association News,* 16 September 1997.)

Rose, Lowell C., and Alec M. Gallup. "The 31st Annual Phi Delta Kappa / Gallup Poll of the Public's Attitudes Toward the Public Schools." *Phi Delta Kappan,* September 1999: 41–56.

Rothman, Robert. *Measuring Up: Standards, Assessment, and School Reform.* San Francisco: Jossey-Bass, 1995.

Rothstein, Richard. *The Way We Were?: The Myths and Realities of America's Student Achievement.* New York: Century Foundation Press, 1998.

Routman, Regie. *Literacy at the Crossroads: Crucial Talk About Reading, Writing, and Other Teaching Dilemmas.* Portsmouth, N.H.: Heinemann, 1996.

Ryan, Richard M., and La Guardia, Jennifer G. "Achievement Motivation Within a Pressured Society: Intrinsic and Extrinsic Motivations to Learn and the Politics of School Reform." In *Advances in Motivation and Achievement,* vol. 11. Stamford, Conn.: JAI Press, 1999.

Sacks, Peter. *Standardized Minds: The High Price of America's Testing Culture and What We Can Do to Change It.* Cambridge, Mass.: Perseus, 1999.

Sahagun, Louis. "L.A. Unified Gets Dismal Ratings from Public." *Los Angeles Times,* 11 April 2000: A1, A22.

Schoen, Harold L., James T. Fey, Christian R. Hirsch, and Arthur F. Coxford. "Issues and Options in the Math Wars." *Phi Delta Kappan,* February 1999: 444–53.

Schrag, Peter. "Too Good to Be True." *The American Prospect,* 3 January 2000.

"Science Leader Criticizes Tests." *FairTest Examiner,* Spring 1998: 8.

Shepard, Lorrie A., and Carribeth L. Bliem. "Parents' Thinking About Standardized Tests and Performance Assessments." *Educational Researcher,* November 1995: 25–32.

Sizer, Theodore R. *Horace's School: Redesigning the American High School.* Boston: Houghton Mifflin, 1992.

Smith, Hilton. "Foxfire Teachers' Networks." In *Democratic Teacher Education: Programs, Processes, Problems, and Prospects*, edited by John M. Novak. Albany: State University of New York Press, 1994.

Steinberg, Jacques. "Academic Standards Eased as a Fear of Failure Spreads." *New York Times*, 3 December 1999: A1, A25.

Stiggins, Richard J. *Student-Centered Classroom Assessment*. New York: Macmillan, 1994.

Taylor, Kathe, and Sherry Walton. *Children at the Center: A Workshop Approach to Standardized Test Preparation, K–8*. Portsmouth, N.H.: Heinemann, 1998.

Van Moorlehem, Tracy. "Students, Parents Rebel Against State Test." *Detroit Free Press*, 29 April 1998: 1–A.

Viadero, Debra. "Stanford Report Questions Accuracy of Tests." *Education Week*, 6 October 1999: 3.

Watson, Marilyn. "The Standards Era and the Moral Goals of Schooling." Paper presented at "Standards and Our Schools" conference, San Jose State Univ., San Jose, Cal., 1998.

Weisman, Jonathan. "Only a Test: The Texas Education Myth." *New Republic*, 10 April 2000: 16–18.

Wellstone, Paul. "High Stakes Tests: A Harsh Agenda for America's Children." Speech delivered at Teachers College, Columbia University, March 31, 2000.

Wiggins, Grant P. *Assessing Student Performance: Exploring the Purpose and Limits of Testing*. San Francisco: Jossey-Bass, 1993.

Wilgoren, Jodi. "Florida's Vouchers a Spur to Two Schools Left Behind." *New York Times*, 14 March 2000: A1, A18.

Wolf, Dennie, Janet Bixby, John Glenn III, and Howard Gardner. "To Use Their Minds Well: Investigating New Forms of Student Assessment." In *Review of Research in Education*, vol. 17, edited by Gerald Grant. Washington, D.C.: American Educational Research Association, 1991.

Wood, Terry, and Patricia Sellers. "Deepening the Analysis: Longitudinal Assessment of a Problem-Centered Mathematics Program." *Journal for Research in Mathematics Education* 28 (1997): 163–86.

Zemelman, Steven, Harvey Daniels, and Arthur Hyde. *Best Practice: New Standards for Teaching and Learning in America's Schools*. 2d ed. Portsmouth, N.H.: Heinemann: 1998.

INDEX